A+ Term Papers

# A+ Term Papers

## Steven Frank

LONGMEADOW
PRESS

Copyright © 1993 by Longmeadow Press

Published by Longmeadow Press, 201 High Ridge Road, Stamford, CT 06904. All rights reserved. No part of this book may be reproduced or utilized in any form or by any means, electronic or mechanical, including photocopying, recording or by any information storage and retrieval system, without permission in writing from the Publisher.

Library of Congress Cataloging-in-Publication Data

Frank, Steven.
    A+ term papers / Steven Frank. — 1st ed.
      p.  cm.
    ISBN 0-681-41194-5 :
    1. Report writing—Handbooks, manuals, etc. 2. Research—Handbooks, manuals, etc.  I. Title.  II. Title: A plus term papers.
LB2369.F73  1993
371.3′028′12—dc20                                      93-2981
                                                            CIP

Printed in United States of America

First Edition

0 9 8 7 6 5 4 3 2 1

# Contents

| | | |
|---|---|---|
| I. | Introduction: What Makes an A+ Term Paper? | 1 |
| II. | Wanted: A Paper Topic | 5 |
| | Variables to Consider | 6 |
| | Fine-Tuning the Topic | 8 |
| III. | What's the Big Idea?: Designing the Thesis Statement | 11 |
| | The Thesis Statement Defined | 11 |
| | Components of the Thesis Statement | 13 |
| IV. | Conducting Research | 15 |
| | Using the Library | 16 |
| | Plan of Attack: Putting Together Your Working Bibliography | 16 |
| | Key Indexes and Bibliographic Sources | 19 |
| | Tracking Down Sources | 21 |
| | Bibliography Cards | 26 |
| V. | Taking Notes | 29 |
| | What to Read For | 30 |
| | Quoting vs. Paraphrasing | 30 |
| | Notes on Primary Texts | 33 |
| | Plagiarism in Notes: A Warning | 33 |
| | The Note Card Method | 34 |
| VI. | Plan of Attack: The Outline | 37 |
| | Shuffling the Deck: Working with the Note Cards | 38 |
| | Standard Outline Format | 39 |
| | Designing Your Outline | 41 |
| | Fine-Tuning the Outline | 43 |

| | | |
|---|---|---|
| VII. | **Paper Structure** | 45 |
| | The Introduction | 46 |
| | The Body | 49 |
| | The Conclusion | 54 |
| | A Final Word on Structure | 56 |
| VIII. | **Paper Format: Documentation, Quotations, and the Bibliography/Works Cited** | 57 |
| | Documenting Sources | 58 |
| | Documentation in the Text of the Paper | 59 |
| | Striving for Clarity; Eliminating Repetition | 64 |
| | Quoting Sources in the Text of the Paper | 66 |
| | Bibliographic and Content Notes | 68 |
| | The Bibliography/Works Cited List | 71 |
| | Typing the Paper | 78 |
| | The Title Page | 78 |
| IX. | **Write Stuff: The Mechanics of Good Writing** | 81 |
| | The Writing Process | 85 |
| | Sentences and Paragraphs: Solid Structure and Smooth Flow | 86 |
| | Watch Out: Common Errors in Grammar and Language Usage | 89 |
| | Language and Style | 93 |

**Appendix A: Sample Outline** — 101
**Appendix B: Sample Paper** — 103
**Appendix C: Sample Bibliography** — 115
**Glossary** — 117

# I.

# Introduction: What Makes an A+ Term Paper?

If you ask most instructors what is exceptional about the papers they give top grades, they won't tell you it's perfect spelling, detailed research, or faultless grammar, although all are parts of a well-written paper. What they'll say that does make a particular term paper an A+ term paper is the quality of the ideas the student expresses in it. Term papers are about communicating ideas. They're not meant to be meaningless writing exercises in which you spit out things you learned in class or cram in as much research as possible to impress your instructor. Rather, they are an opportunity to demonstrate your mastery of the subject. In writing a paper, your goal should be no less than to become an expert on your chosen topic, with something significant and intelligent to say.

Do not underestimate the importance of the ideas you put into your paper. A paper can be beautifully written and carefully researched, yet without interesting ideas it will be empty, unimpressive, and boring. The kind of paper that gets an A+ is one that packs a punch—one that is provocative, sophisticated, and original. To write this kind of paper, you need to center it on a powerful argument of some kind, one that is distinctly your own. Without a central argument, your paper will not differ from an encyclopedia entry or a chapter in a textbook—it will just become a bunch of random facts strung together.

This does not mean, however, that writing and research are not important. If you cannot express your ideas so that your reader can understand them, they will not amount to much. Always remember: your reader can't see inside your head; it's up to you to get your ideas out on paper and present them in a way that your reader can understand and appreciate them. That's what good writing is all about—communicating ideas. Equally important is the research you conduct in the process of writing your paper. Research is necessary to support your claims.

When you're writing a paper, don't think of yourself as a student working away at a school project. Think of yourself as a lawyer arguing an important case before a judge. By the trial's end, you want the judge (your instructor) to be absolutely convinced of your case, beyond any reasonable doubt. Like a lawyer, you'll present facts and evidence to support your case, in a clear, orderly, and persuasive fashion. And you'll want to argue your case as if somebody's life is on the line, filling each sentence with passion and meaning.

Coming up with ideas is hard work; it takes time and effort. This book will give some suggestions to help you come up with ideas, but it won't come up with them for you. No book can. What this book will do is help you to present your ideas in a manner that will best show them off. Organization is the key to effective research and to good writing, and it begins from the moment you begin work on your paper. By taking you step by step through the process of writing a paper—from settling on a topic to proofreading the final draft—this book will ensure that your work proceeds efficiently and productively. Moreover, this book includes important information concerning the proper format and structure of an effective research paper.

This book describes guidelines for writing a standard research paper, the kind most often required for student courses, and can be valuable both to high school and college-level students. Although a college research paper will be written on a more advanced level, the elements of an effective term paper and the procedure for writing one do not differ between the high school and college levels. Many high school teachers insist that the student follow the method taught to them in class. While the writing method that various instructors teach might differ slightly from the one described here, the guidelines and tips included here can still be enormously helpful in writing a paper.

We'll begin by discussing how to come up with topics and, especially important, how to design the thesis statement—the central argument that will serve as the main point for your paper. Next we'll examine various means of conducting and organizing research, from where to find source materials to tips on keeping track of the information you gather so you can effectively bring it into the paper. From there, we'll concentrate on the structure of a term paper and see how it works not only to make your ideas clear to the reader but also to make your argument more powerful.

This book also includes an important section highlighting the basics of research paper format, detailing the specifics of how to cite the source materials you will bring in to support your argument. Format is an extremely important part of writing a research paper; it makes your paper clean and easy-to-read and, especially important, protects you from committing plagiarism. Finally, this book presents valuable tips that will help make your paper a solid piece of good writing. At the end of the book, an actual research paper is included, enabling you to see these principles put into action.

Writing a term paper need not be a meaningless drill that you complete merely for the sake of fulfilling a requirement. Like the term paper itself, the experience of writing the paper depends on what you put into it. It will be a burden only if you let it be. Ten years from now, the grade on the paper won't matter; what you learn from writing it, however, can stay with you for a lifetime.

So try to make this an A+ writing *experience*. That's the grade that really counts.

# II.

# Wanted:
# A Paper Topic

Choosing the topic can often be the most difficult and challenging part of writing a research paper. In settling upon a particular subject, there are many things to take into consideration that will inevitably affect the quality of your work. When you choose a topic, you also, to a large extent, determine the final product. It's pretty safe to say that a crucial requirement for an original paper is starting with an original topic. So make certain to give this part of the process ample time, effort, and thought.

How much consideration goes into choosing your topic depends on the kind of assignment you receive from your instructor. Assignments vary; some instructors assign specific topics, while others merely suggest topics. Sometimes an instructor will give the students freedom to decide their own topics.

For those of you who have already received a topic from your instructor, don't think that means you can skip ahead to the next section. Even with the most rigidly defined topic, you are going to have plenty of room to maneuver on your own. In this case, the challenge is to view the subject from your own point of view and to somehow make it your own. Many of the guidelines included here will be of help to you as well.

Many students, until they learn better, believe that when they are allowed to choose their own topics it makes writing the paper a breeze. They quickly learn that having free reign, while exciting, can also be overwhelming. There are infinite possibilities for topics, and choosing one can seem like picking a needle from a haystack. So, where do you begin?

## Variables to Consider

In settling on a topic, it is crucial to take into account certain variables that if not considered ahead of time can lead to all kinds of stumbling blocks later on. In deciding your topic, be certain to consider the following:

**1. Let Yourself Fall in Love.** When you choose your topic, keep in mind that you are going to be married to this subject for a long, long time. As with any marriage, if you love and respect your partner, the day-to-day details are smoother. The number one rule for deciding your topic is: *Choose something that interests you.* Find a subject you want to know more about, perhaps something that perplexes or challenges you. Whatever it is, make certain you won't become bored with it in a day or two but will continue to enjoy reading and writing about it at length.

**2. Be Unique.** Depending upon your instructor, you might also want to choose a topic that is somewhat unusual. Most instructors respect and appreciate the additional effort and risk involved in trying to be unique. If everyone else is writing about Shakespeare's *Hamlet,* for example, then maybe you should write about *The Tempest.* Or if you do want to write about *Hamlet,* try to pick an aspect of it that is different, one not particularly obvious or often commented upon. Writing about something unusual or from a different perspective will make the paper more stimulating for you to research and write and more interesting for your reader to read.

It may seem very difficult to be original when you are writing about topics such as historical events or literary works that have been discussed repeatedly by others. But remember the story of the blind men and the elephant: one man feels the trunk and thinks the elephant is a snake; another feels a leg and thinks it is a tree. People always view a subject from their own point of view. There are many ways to see the same elephant—and to write about it. In your paper, try to bring your own perspective to bear upon the topic.

**3. Instructor/Reader Expectations.** A good writer will always address his or her work to the proper audience. An author of a children's story, for example, is going to write in a completely different manner than someone writing a medical school text book.

With most term papers, the primary audience will be the instructor (or other members of the class). It is therefore extremely important that you understand what the instructor expects from you. Before you begin work, make certain you fully understand the assignment and that you are aware of all the specifics involved. Ask your instructor questions: How much research should you be conducting? How long should the paper be? What format should you use? It can be enormously frustrating to write a wonderful paper but be penalized for not following instructions.

Abiding by requirements is a part of being a writer. All writers are forced to write within certain guidelines: reporters often have to write what their editors assign; lawyers have to follow very specific formats when writing legal briefs, etc. By having to write according to certain limitations in your term paper, you are learning how to write in a professional manner. You will also discover ways to fulfill requirements but at the same time maintain your originality and creativity.

**4. Trying It On For Size.** Anyone who has heard the story of "Goldilocks and the Three Bears" knows an important aspect of choosing a paper topic—you don't want one that's too big or too small, but one that is just right. When you choose your topic, it is extremely important that you consider the length requirements of the paper *before* you have begun writing. Term papers are meant to be detailed, in-depth studies within a particular field. To ensure that you will write an airtight, solid, and effective term paper, you need to choose a topic that you can address fully and comprehensively in the amount of space you have been given by the instructor.

If you choose a topic that is too big for the paper's length, you will be forced to write about it in superficial terms, without any depth, concentration, or focus. It would be difficult, for example, to write a paper on "The Plays of William Shakespeare" in a ten- or twenty-page term paper; you would have to discuss most of the plays in less than half a page, making it impossible to go into any kind of detail.

Additionally, by choosing too broad a topic, you run the risk of biting off more than you can chew in terms of research. To research all the plays of William Shakespeare would take a lifetime. You want to be certain that whatever topic you decide upon, you'll be able to sample a substantial amount of the available studies and research so that you'll be fully informed of the field in which you are writing.

Students too often worry about "filling up" pages. To many, a ten- or twenty-page term paper seems like being asked to write a novel. In fear that they will not be able to fill up the space, these students inevitably choose a topic that is much too broad. *Don't worry about filling up the pages.* If you conduct enough research and give your topic the kind of thought you should, you'll have plenty of material to fill your paper. In fact, you may have difficulty determining what to edit out!

Choosing a topic that is too small is also something to watch out for. If you choose a topic that is too narrow for an entire term paper, you'll wind up bending over backwards to fill up the space. Your paper will be too wordy, lacking precision and concentration. A twenty-page paper on the character of the night watchman in *Hamlet* would probably run out of steam pretty quickly and fizzle out. Your topic should be big enough so that you can fill your paper with rich ideas that will keep your reader engaged to the last word.

Choosing a topic appropriate for the amount of space takes experience. Eventually, you'll have a better idea of what an appropriate topic is for a particular paper length. For now, be careful to avoid the extremes—too broad or too narrow—because they will be the most difficult to adjust to once you have begun writing. With most other topics, once you have written a rough draft, you'll probably be able to edit or expand in order to meet the page requirements.

Through trial and error, you'll eventually become skilled at choosing a topic that, in the words of that golden-haired heroine, is "just right."

## Fine-Tuning the Topic

Although choosing a topic that is too broad is a danger, it is certainly acceptable to think in broad terms when you are initially considering topics. People don't pull innovative and highly specified topics out of thin air. Good topics are the product of a lengthy investigative period. Beginning with some general subject matter, you must do some preliminary reading and devote ample thinking time in order to fine-tune a topic.

The first step in deciding a topic is to choose a very general subject that interests you. Think about the topics you studied in class. Was there a particular subject that you enjoyed learning about? Was there anything you only touched on in class but that you wanted to learn more about? How about something you read that challenged you? Was there anything that touched a nerve? Sparked other ideas?

Here is a list of general subjects that would make a good starting point:

- A particular work of literature, article or text, or a body of works, you read in your class.
- An author, person, or particular group of individuals you studied in your course.
- A historical period or event (the Roaring Twenties, Civil War, Classical Greece) or a contemporary news event (the end of the Cold War, the 1992 Presidential Campaign).
- A literary period, genre, or combination of the two (Neoclassicism, Modern Drama, Romantic Poetry).
- A scientific field or subfield, either in the general sciences or the social sciences (Computer Science and Technology, Criminal Psychology).
- A particular issue, either historical or contemporary (Prohibition, Women's Rights).

Notice that all are generalized subject matters that would require exhaustive research and lengthy papers in order to be fully examined. Therefore they are not appropriate for term paper topics and must be narrowed down and fine-tuned.

Once you have chosen a general subject or field, the next step is to immerse yourself in it. Begin reading anything you can get your hands on that relates to the subject. At this point, a trip to the library is called for. The most effective place to begin is probably the reference room, where many general sources and resources are kept. Reference books cannot be checked out and must remain in the library. Although this forces you to work in the library, it also ensures that some resources will definitely be there to help you. A reference librarian is usually available who can suggest general reading for you. An encyclopedia (*Encyclopedia Britannica, Encyclopedia Americana, Collier's Encyclopedia*) might be an excellent place to start with a preliminary reading as it will give you an overview of your topic.

In the reference room, you'll be able to find many specialized dictionaries and encyclopedias that specifically address certain fields and subjects, including: Arts and Entertainment (Music, Dance, Theater, Film); Science and Technology (Astronomy, Biology, Chemistry, Computer Science, Geology, Physics); Economics; Education; History (American, European, World); Literature; Mathematics; Psychology; Religion; Social Sciences.

As you read, something will start to happen; bells will go off, lightbulbs will flash, and you'll start coming up with your own interests and ideas. Don't expect it to happen immediately; that's not the way the human mind works. You need to immerse yourself in a subject and allow it to percolate in your mind for a period of time. As you gain an intimate understanding of the subject, you'll begin making connections with things you've learned, seeing things from your own viewpoint, and conceiving your own opinions.

Make certain you keep track of any ideas that pop into your head. Keep a pad of paper with you and jot down all your thoughts. As you continue to read, your interests will become more focused and defined. At the same time, you will naturally begin narrowing down your topic into something more specific and original.

# III.

# What's the Big Idea?: Designing the Thesis Statement

## The Thesis Statement Defined

The heart of any research paper is the thesis statement. It is the paper's main idea, usually some kind of theory, argument, or viewpoint that stems from the general topic and is proven in the body of the paper. It serves as the paper's backbone, holding together all the parts of the paper in a cohesive whole.

The thesis statement is not the same thing as your topic, although they are closely related. Following the steps in the last chapter, you will have come up with a topic, such as "Imagery in Hamlet" or "U.S. Intelligence During World War II." Within this general topic, you will now formulate a more specific idea that addresses a particular aspect or reflects a particular point of view of the topic. You will then condense this idea into a single statement that sums up the central idea of the paper: this is the thesis statement.

While a topic is usually objective, a thesis will reflect your impression of the subject material and therefore be more subjective. All writing represents someone's interpretation, and all interpretations are open to discussion and alternate viewpoints. Your thesis statement represents your interpretation of a particular topic.

Observe the differences between the following topics and the thesis statements that ultimately may emerge from them:

## Topics

American Literature after World War I
Madness in Shakespeare's Plays
The Vietnam War in Popular Films
Cardiovascular Exercise and Health
Structuring of Eugene O'Neill's Plays
The Effectiveness of the Two-Party System of Government
The Impact of the Environment on the Economy

## Thesis Statements

- American literature written during the 1920s reflects the prevailing anxieties and fears of the postwar period.

- Madness in Shakespeare's tragedies is both a symptom and cause of the tragic circumstances in which characters find themselves.

- The tone of popular films set in Vietnam has become increasingly more negative, indicating a shift in popular opinion of the war.

- Diet has been shown to have a more significant impact on blood pressure than cardiovascular exercise.

- The structure of *Long Day's Journey into Night* draws out and enhances the intricate interactions of the Tyrone family.

- The American two-party system of government no longer fulfills the purposes for which it was originally intended and is doomed to extinction.

- The rapid depletion of the rain forest, if not addressed now, will result in a severe global economic crisis.

All the thesis statements are subjective points of view that must be supported by evidence and research. You cannot argue "American Literature after World War

I," but you can argue that "American literature after World War I reflected people's anxieties."

Not all thesis statements are necessarily controversial or completely subjective arguments. Many research papers are primarily written to describe or present materials concerning a particular subject. However, because these papers still have a purpose and a central idea that the writer wants to express, they must have a thesis statement or they will be unfocused pages of writing with no point. *Every paper should have some kind of thesis statement,* even if it merely summarizes the main point of the paper.

Most instructors, however, in assigning a term paper are not looking for a general description of the subject but for your thoughts and ideas about it. To write a paper that will knock your instructor's socks off, you want to have as interesting and thoughtful a thesis possible. The more original the thesis statement, the more original your paper. Don't be afraid to be daring and even a bit controversial. But talk to your instructor about the assignment to make sure you are writing the kind of paper he or she expects.

## Components of the Thesis Statement

An effective thesis statement should do the following:

**1. Be specific.** As you can see from reading the examples above, thesis statements are extremely concentrated and narrowly defined. Being so specific, they ensure that papers will remain focused and not veer off into unrelated territory that distracts the reader.

**2. Reflect your own ideas.** Research papers are meant to express your thoughts and ideas. Although you will be using sources to prove your point, your thesis should be entirely your own, phrased in your own language, and reflect your own outlook on the subject matter.

**3. Be something you believe.** Unlike a lawyer, you do have some choice in the cases you argue (as an exercise, an instructor might occasionally assign a topic that will force you to argue a viewpoint with which you don't necessarily agree). Don't work against the grain and argue something that you do not actually believe. If you are arguing your beliefs, the paper will bear the strength of your personal convictions.

**4. Be something you can successfully prove.** Your goal in writing the paper is to convince the reader of your theory, idea, or viewpoint beyond a shadow of a doubt. Therefore, make certain you pick a thesis you know you can prove.

You probably won't know until after you've done some research whether or not you can prove the thesis. After conducting research, you may find there just isn't enough evidence to support your idea. You might even find yourself becoming convinced of the opposite argument. As long as you allow yourself enough time to complete the paper, you can still change your thesis statement in the initial stages of research.

Before you begin researching your paper, it is not crucial to have set your thesis statement. After all, to argue something conclusively, you need to gather evidence, which is what the research process is all about. But you should have some general idea as to what you think your thesis will be so that your research will be directed. As you conduct research and gain more knowledge of your topic, you'll continue to hone your thesis statement.

One more point: once you have an idea of what your thesis statement will be, it is always a good idea to discuss it with your instructor. This will make certain whether or not you're on the right track. Your instructor may also have suggestions for you in terms of doing research.

# IV.

# Conducting Research

Most term papers are research papers, which means that the writer utilizes outside sources. There are two kinds of sources: *primary* and *secondary*. Primary sources are the ones you focus on in your paper, those specific works that you analyze and discuss, such as works of literature, historical documents, or essays and articles on certain theories and philosophies. Primary sources can also be data obtained in a scientific study. Secondary sources are books and articles by critics, historians, scholars, and other writers who comment on and address the primary sources.

Primary and secondary sources will serve as the evidence that supports your thesis statement, and you will bring them into your paper to prove your own ideas and theories. However, they are not meant to take the place of your ideas and become the primary focus of the paper.

This chapter details the two main parts of research: first, how to compile a list of sources you would like to examine for your paper; and second, where to find these sources once you do.

## Using the Library

The library is the most important tool you have to help you write your paper, and it is important that you learn how to use it to your advantage. Much more than a resting home for books, the library is a place abundant in different kinds of resources that can be enormously helpful.

Think of the library as your office while you work on your paper, and take the time to learn your way around. Get the feel of the place so that you will feel comfortable working there. Take advantage of the tours or orientation programs many libraries offer. The better you know your surroundings, the more time you'll save when doing the work.

Don't be intimidated by the library. It's there as a service to help you. Never be afraid to ask the librarians questions. That's their job, and they'll be only too happy to help you.

Try to use the best library available. A college or university library will probably have a more extensive collection and better resources than a local public library. The main branch of the public library in most cities will also have an extensive collection of sources and varied services.

## Plan of Attack: Putting Together Your Working Bibliography

Libraries contain a wealth of information, but it will not fall into your lap. It is up to you to find what you need. As with any quest, you must have some idea of what you are looking for before you begin your search.

This is why you should first compile a working bibliography. A working bibliography is simply a list of sources that you plan to examine for possible use in your paper. It serves as a road map that will help you navigate as you search for sources for your paper. It will eventually develop into your final bibliography—also known as the Works Cited—which will appear at the end of your completed paper and list all the sources you have included in your paper.

# Sources for the Working Bibliography

There are several ways to find possible sources for your paper. As you read of various sources you would like to consult, be certain to write down the information you need, preferably on bibliography cards (see pg. 18).

You can use any or all of the following resources:

**1. The Subject Catalog:** Libraries index all their books in a catalog, either on cards or on computer disk, with separate entries for Author, Title, and Subject (see Catalogs section in this chapter for more information on this). You can find many possible sources for your paper by either consulting the subject cards in the card catalog or by conducting a search by subject on the on-line computer.

Most libraries organize their subject catalog according to the list of standard subjects set by the Library of Congress, although a few libraries use their own subject classifications. The library should have a subject list available for you to consult. Check the list of subjects that the library uses to classify its books and identify the subject heading within which your topic will fall. Entries are often further divided into subcategories, particularly the on-line computer catalogs. For example, the *Literature* heading might be divided into various historical periods and genres.

Next, scan the titles in the catalog within that subject or subcategory, looking for any that seem interesting, relevant, or helpful. You will probably not be able to consult all the sources listed within the subject heading and will somehow have to narrow down your list. You may be able to tell from the titles how relevant a particular source will be for your paper. Anthologies and collections of essays are especially helpful sources, particularly when you begin conducting research, because they will give you a sampling of secondary resources within one book.

**2. Reference Books and Bibliographic Sources:** There are many published bibliographies that list books and various sources (often including academic journals and periodical articles) on a single subject. For example, there is a separate published bibliography for almost every one of Shakespeare's plays that lists secondary sources only for that play. For many subjects, there will be some kind of bibliography that addresses that specific topic.

Bibliographies compile citations for various books and sources. A citation is a bibliographic listing for a particular source that provides key information (author, title, and publication information), which will help you locate the source. Annotated bibliographies are especially helpful because they also list a brief description for each source included. Here is a sample annotated citation:

> Rabkin, Norman. *Shakespeare and the Common Understanding.*
> New York: Free Press, 1967. 267 pp.
> The true constant of Shakespearean tragedy is the dialectical dramaturgy, and *King Lear* provides one of the most powerful examples. The universe envisioned by the stage world is subject to contradictory interpretations....

Bibliographies are usually located in the reference section of the library. To find a bibliography on your topic, you can either ask the reference librarian for suggestions or use the catalog. Under many of the subjects in the subject catalog, there will be a subcategory that lists bibliographies for that subject.

In order to find periodical sources, you can use specialized indexes, which primarily list citations for journal and magazine articles and essays within larger works. The indexes will list the articles, usually by subject. Abstracts are a type of index that will also include a brief description or excerpt from each article or essay listed.

As with bibliographies, there are general indexes as well as specialized indexes that cover specific topics in periodical guides. The index will list a citation for an article, displaying the key information on the source, such as the author, title of the periodical in which it can be found, the periodical's year, volume, and issue number, and the pages where the article can be found. Most magazine and journal titles are abbreviated; a key to the abbreviations will be at the front of the index.

Here is a sample journal citation:

*Author* — Raleigh, John Henry.
*Title* — "Communal, Familial, and Personal Memories in O'Neill's *Long Day's Journey Into Night*."
*Journal Title (Abbreviated)* — MD.
*Date* — 1988 Mar.;
*Volume #* — 31
*Issue #* — (1).
*Pages* — 63–72.
*Annotation* — [Treatment of memory; relationship to Irish-American experience.]

**3. Bibliographies in Sources:** Most academic books, essays, and journal articles include their own bibliographies listing the sources the author has used. These also can be very helpful sources for your paper. Each time you read a new book or article, be certain to check the author's bibliography and notes to see if there is anything you might like to consult for your own paper.

**4. Computerized Information Resources:** Several of the bibliographies and indexes listed below, such as the *MLA Bibliography* and the *Reader's Guide to Periodic Literature,* are now also available on computer data bases. Many libraries have computers with access to various bibliographic data bases that you can use to conduct on-line searches. When you conduct an on-line search, you instruct the computer to search for sources relating to a particular author, title, or subject, and the computer will put together and print out a bibliography for you.

Libraries have different regulations for conducting on-line searches. Some might require that you purchase time on the computer or that you meet with a librarian to learn the system before using it on your own. In some libraries, the public is not allowed to conduct on-line searches. You must fill out a request form in order to have the search conducted for you, and there may be a waiting period before you receive a printout of the bibliography. (This is not to be confused with the on-line catalog, which is always free and open to the public.)

# Key Indexes and Bibliographic Sources

What follows is a listing of some of the major indexes and bibliographies that might be helpful in your search for sources. Most can be found in the reference room of any library. Remember, these are only general indexes. Many other bibliographies are tailored to specific subjects, topics, and fields that might match your particular topic.

### Arts, Humanities, and Literature

*Annual Bibliography of English Language and Literature*   An index of secondary sources for all literature in English, categorized by century. New editions are published every year.

*Humanities Index*   An index of articles appearing in approximately 350 academic journals and some popular periodicals in the humanities. Categorizes articles by theme, genre, author, and topic, and includes a listing of book and theater reviews. Updated quarterly.

*MLA International Bibliography of Books and Articles on the Modern Languages and Literatures*   An extremely comprehensive listing of secondary sources for literature from all periods, the MLA (Modern Language Association) Bibliography indexes books, articles in journals, and essays in anthologies and compilations. Although it contains an abundance of information, the MLA Bibliography has undergone several format changes and is therefore somewhat complicated to use.

- From 1981 to the present, the MLA is divided into two books: the Classified List with an Author Index (to authors of sources) and the Subject List.

The Classified List is divided into sections ("volumes") that refer to general categories of subjects: Volume I-II (National Literatures: by country, century, and author); Volume III (Linguistics); Volume IV (General Literature: studies and theories on general literature); Volume V (Folklore: arranged by genres).

The Subject List does not include full citations. However, it will show where particular subjects might be cross-listed in other sections.

Try to consult both the Subject and Classified lists.

- For 1969 to 1980, the MLA is contained in one volume and does not have a subject index. It is organized in three sections: Volume I (General, English, American, Commonwealth, Latin, Celtic, Folklore); Volume II (European, Asian, African, and Latin American); Volume III (Linguistics and Languages).
- Before 1969, the MLA is contained in one volume but is not split into three sections. The listings are organized by category within the single volume.
- Before 1956, the MLA lists only articles by Americans. For other authors, consult other bibliographies.

## Biography

*Biography and Genealogy Master Index* Does not include biographical information on personalities but indexes biographical sources and studies.

*Biography Index* Lists books and over 2,000 periodicals on various biographical sources, with a subject index. Updated quarterly.

*Who's Who* Lists key information (date of birth, education, spouse, children, occupations, title, etc.) regarding various prominent personalities. There are several different versions of *Who's Who*, including American and International editions.

## General

*Books in Print* A listing of all books still in print and currently published in the United States, separated by author, subject, title, publisher, and forthcoming titles. Published annually.

*Essay and General Literature Index* An index to essays that appear in books of collected essays and anthologies in the fields of the humanities and social sciences. Organized by author and subject. Updated semiannually.

*Reader's Guide to Periodical Literature* This is the primary index to articles in popular magazines. Approximately 200 different magazines (general, news, entertainment, popular interest, etc.) are indexed. Organized by subject and author. Updated biweekly.

## History

*Historical Abstracts* An index to over 2,000 historical journals, covering the historical period from 1450 to the present.

*International Bibliography of Historical Sciences* An index to books and articles on all historical periods.

### Current Events
*Facts on File* Includes summaries of major news events, national and international, indexed by subject. Updated weekly.

*Newspaper Indexes* Many major newspapers, such as the *New York Times* and *Wall Street Journal,* have their own indexes, which will often be organized by subject heading. There is also a *National Newspaper Index* that incorporates several major newspapers in one index.

Indexes to book and theater reviews in certain newspapers, such as the *New York Times* and *London Times,* are also available.

### Sciences
*General Science Index* An index of articles appearing in academic journals and periodicals from all fields in the general sciences. Updated quarterly.

*Social Sciences Index* An index of articles appearing in academic journals and some periodicals in the social sciences, organized by subject and author, with a separate listing of book reviews. Updated quarterly.

# Tracking Down Sources

To track down most sources in the library you need to learn how to use the library's central catalog. Most libraries have their catalogs on cards, but more and more libraries are also storing their files on computer disk, which is known as the on-line catalog.

## Card Catalogs

The information in the card catalog is usually indexed by Author, Title, and Subject. In most libraries, the author and title cards will be grouped together in the same area, and the subject cards will be found in a different section of drawers. In other libraries, the author, title, and subject cards will all be grouped together alphabetically within the same catalog.

For each book in the library, there will be a separate author, title, and subject card in the catalog. This enables you to find a book even if you do not have all the information about it. For example, you may know the title of a certain work but do not remember the author. By using the title cards, you will still be able to find the book. Similarly, you may want to see what works a particular author has written.

By examining the author cards, you will be able to see titles of all the books by that author that are in the library.

The subject category is especially helpful when you begin your quest for sources. It enables you to look for information even if you do not have a particular book in mind. Most libraries organize their subject catalog according to the list of standard subjects set by the Library of Congress, although some libraries may use their own subject classifications. The library should have a subject list available that you can consult. After identifying the subject under which your topic falls, you can then look in the subject catalog to find whatever books the library has on that subject.

The cards in the catalog all detail basic information about the book, including author, title, subject, publication information, author's date of birth, and number of pages. Most important, the card will also indicate the book's location within the library. Most libraries are organized according to either the Dewey decimal system or the Library of Congress system. These systems use combinations of numbers and letters to indicate a book's subject and location in the library. In the card catalog, a combination of letters and numbers will appear in the top left-hand corner of the card. This is known as the call number, and it is based upon the system of organization the library uses. Each book within the library has a call number, and you use it to track down the book (see "Searching the Stacks" below). Always be certain to copy down the call number.

# The On-Line Catalog

Many libraries are now also putting their central catalogs onto a computer database known as the on-line catalog. In libraries that have an on-line catalog, there will usually be several computer terminals, close to the card catalog, to which the public has access. Most on-line systems are very easy to use and do not require much computer knowledge. There will probably be instructions by the terminals or a HELP function on the keyboard that will show you what to do. As with anything in the library, you can always ask a librarian for help. Once you become familiar with the on-line catalog, you'll find it is much easier and faster to use than the card catalog.

As with the card catalog, an on-line catalog is also broken down by author, title, and subject. In most on-line systems, the first step will be to indicate whether you wish to conduct your search by author, title, or subject. Different computer systems use different commands and codes that you will use to indicate how you want to proceed. Again, the HELP function or some kind of written instructions should be available.

Once you have indicated how you want to conduct your search, a prompt will appear on the screen requesting you to enter the author, title, or subject for which you are searching.

One advantage of using the on-line system is that you do not usually need full information on the source in order to conduct a search. For example, if you enter an author's last name, the screen will display a list of full names for all authors with that last name, sometimes with their dates of birth. This information can help you pinpoint the right author. When you have selected a name from the list, the screen will then display a list of works by that author.

In many libraries' computer catalogs, you do not even need to know the full title of a work in order to find it. You can begin a search just by entering key words from the title. The screen will then display all the titles that have those key words in it. For example, if you are looking for *Portrait of the Artist as a Young Man,* but do not remember the exact title, you can type in the word *Portrait.* The screen will then display all titles in the library that begin with the word *Portrait* (so not only will *Portrait of the Artist* appear but *Portrait of a Lady* as well).

To conduct a subject search, you must enter a subject heading from the library's list of subject classifications or the computer system will not recognize the command. Consult the list of subjects in order to find the one most relevant to your topic. The system may then allow you to choose from subcategories within the subject, making your search easier.

Once you have selected the title you are interested in, a screen will appear that will display the same information that is included in the card catalog. The primary advantage of using the on-line catalog is that in addition to displaying general information about the book and the book's location, it will also indicate the status of the book. The screen might show if the book is in the library, on loan, or missing, and, in some cases, when the book is due back.

Many on-line catalogs will enable you to print out hard copies of the information that appears on the screen. This can be extremely helpful both for tracking down sources and for when you later prepare your bibliography.

## Searching the Stacks

The bulk of the library's resources consists of books that are housed in "stacks," meaning on the shelves. In most libraries, the public has access to the stacks. After you have copied the book's call number, from either the card catalog or the on-line catalog, you can then find the book in the stacks. You can then either ask a librarian where it will be or try to track it down yourself.

In some libraries, the public is denied access to the stacks. In these libraries, you should fill out a request slip with the call number and give it to the librarian. The book will then be retrieved for you.

Most libraries are organized according to either the Dewey decimal system or the Library of Congress system (used in most colleges and universities).

The Dewey decimal system groups books according to ten major headings, each one given its own number. The first few digits of a book's call number, listed before the decimal point, will indicate this subject heading and will give you an idea of the general section of the library in which the book will be shelved. The digits following the decimal point more specifically indicate the exact location of the book.

Once you are in the general area, the books will be shelved in numerical order. There should be cards or signs that indicate the range of call numbers in each row of shelves. The numbers will be printed on the books' spines, and you search down the row until you match the call number.

The Library of Congress system is organized in a similar manner but separates books into twenty major categories, each one given a letter or combination of letters. The first few letters in the call number will indicate the subject and the general area in which the book will be shelved, while the later digits will more specifically indicate the book's exact location.

If a book is not located where it should be, do not necessarily give up your search. Libraries are busy places and people are constantly shuffling books around the shelves. Look for the book in the surrounding area, checking other shelves; look at books lying around or near the location; and look on nearby desks, tables, and book carts.

If you still cannot find the book and it is a vital source for your paper, go to the circulation desk and ask for help. The librarian may be able to check if the book has been returned but has not yet been shelved, or tell you when it is due back. Some libraries will allow you to put a book on reserve, which means that when the book is returned, it will be held aside for you and you will be notified. Some libraries, especially at colleges and universities, can have a book recalled if it has been out longer than the due date.

## Other Book Locations

Not all books will be located in the general stacks. Many might be in the reference section of the library. Reference books must remain in the library and may not be checked out. The call number will usually be preceded by REF or R in order to indicate that the book is a reference book, shelved in the reference section of the library.

Oversized books are also often shelved separately. The catalog entry should indicate if a book is oversize. You can then ask a librarian where the oversize books are shelved.

In university libraries, professors often put books on reserve, which means that they are kept in a separate section so that students in that course may borrow the book for a limited amount of time. In this case, the catalog entry should say "On Reserve." You can go to the reserve desk and ask to see the book.

# Other Resources in the Library

In addition to books, libraries house many other research materials, including newspapers, magazines, journals, videotapes, audiotapes, and maps. These materials will usually be kept within their own sections, which will often be indicated in the catalog entry. You can ask the librarian or check the library directory to find where these materials are located.

Magazines, periodicals, and scholarly journals are sometimes bound together in volumes and shelved in the stacks. (This is why bibliographies list a volume number in addition to the date of a periodical.) Bound volumes will usually be grouped in the same area in the library.

Due to the enormous space newspapers and magazines would consume and the problems of decay, libraries keep them only for a limited time period. Current newspapers and periodicals are usually kept in a separate area or room.

After a certain period of time, newspapers and most journals and magazines are transformed to a microform. Through a special process, the entire newspaper or magazine is miniaturized and transferred to film. This process enables enormous amounts of paper to be stored within a very small space. There are various types of microform, the most popular being *microfilm,* a long, thin strip of film that is rolled up, and *microfiche,* which is a single, transparent sheet.

The microforms are usually kept in a separate microform room. If a catalog entry says "MICRO," or if you know you are looking for a periodical or journal that would be on microform, go directly to the microform room. A librarian will usually be there to help you. In most libraries, you need a librarian to get the microform for you, although in some you can get them yourself from a file cabinet. Make certain you know the exact date of the periodical so that you can find the right microform.

As a result of the miniaturization process, the print on microforms is too small to see with the naked eye. In order to read the material, you need to use a special monitor, which will probably be in the same room in which the microforms are kept. There are usually a limited number of monitors and you will often have to wait. Find out if there is a sign-up sheet. The first few times you work on a monitor, you will probably need a librarian to show you how to use it.

Some specially equipped monitors will enable you to make photocopies of different pages as they appear on the screen. You may want to use one of these machines since it is easier to take notes from paper than read off a screen. Having copies also enables you to spend more time with the source on your own.

Audiotapes and videotapes are often classified according to their own system. The library might have a separate catalog, brochure, or booklet listing titles, subjects, and artists that you can consult.

Conducting Research

## Interlibrary Loans

If the library you are using does not have a particular source, don't despair. Many libraries provide a service whereby they will borrow a source from another library (usually at a minimal fee). Ask at the circulation desk or in the reference library how you can get an interlibrary loan.

## Looking for Sources Outside the Library

If you cannot find a particular source at your local library, you might consider purchasing the book. Call several bookstores, particularly college bookstores or those that specialize in used books, to see if they carry the book or can order it for you. You can also try calling the publisher to special order it. One volume of *Books in Print* lists publishers with addresses and phone numbers. You can also approach your instructor, who might own the very source for which you are so desperately searching. At the least, the instructor should be able to make suggestions to help you find it.

## Bibliography Cards

As you find out about or track down possible sources, it is extremely important that you keep track of all pertinent bibliographic information because you will need it for your final bibliography. It saves a great deal of time and energy to get this information when you first examine the sources rather than having to return to the library and track them down later. While you may keep bibliographic information in list form on notepaper or legal pads, it is highly recommended that you fill out bibliography cards.

Bibliography cards make it much easier to keep track of the many sources you are examining and ultimately make writing your final bibliography much simpler. For each source, you fill out a separate index card with the publication information about the source. The cards therefore provide greater flexibility, enabling you to order or arrange them in a way that is convenient to you, such as alphabetical order or order of importance. You can also group various cards together to make your research more organized, such as according to various locations in the library, sources that you still need to consult, or articles that come from the same original source. The cards also give you room to make notes to yourself that will help in your research, such as where you discovered the source, the source's location in the library, the call number, etc.

As you discard various sources for whatever reason, you can place those cards in a separate pile. When you have completed your paper, you then need only alphabetize the remaining cards and you will have your final bibliography.

You can fill out bibliography cards either when you originally read of a source, such as in the subject catalog or in an index or abstract, or when you have found the actual source. At the top of each card, copy the publication information in the correct bibliographic format (discussed in Chapter VIII on Paper Format). By getting in the habit of writing information in the bibliographic format when you first locate a source, you ensure that you will have all the required information and will not have to return to the library to recheck sources.

When you look up a book in the catalog, write the call number in the upper corner of the card, so that you can then locate the book in the library. You can also write the source's general location in the library, such as the microform room, reference library, etc. At the bottom, leave space for additional notes on the source, such as your source for this bibliographic information or particular points you want to check in it.

Because you will probably be reading a large number of sources, it is suggested that you also write a brief summary of each work you read. These summaries will be especially helpful if you later need to return to a particular source in order to find a specific point. Either at the bottom or on the back of the bibliography card, write a one- or two-line summation of the article or book. What seems to be the purpose of the material? What is it seeking to prove? See if you can identify the source's thesis statement and write that down. Beneath it, you might also want to list the essential points that the source makes. (You might want to use the larger size index cards to give you room to do this.)

## Sample Bibliography Card with Summary:

Abrams, M. H.                                    PN603.A3
    Natural Supernaturalism: Tradition and Revolution in Romantic Literature.
    New York: Norton, 1971.
-Located in general stacks (look for Shelley chapter).
SUMMARY: The Romantic writers reformulated supernatural and mystical religious beliefs into nature.
KEY POINTS: -Discusses Christian scheme to history.
-Begins with Wordsworth and goes into detail about how various writers secularized Christian doctrines in their works.

# V.

## Taking Notes

When you've tracked down a particular source, glance through the book or article and try to determine if it is something you would like to examine at length. Read the preface or introduction of a book, or the first few paragraphs of an article or essay. Try to determine the main argument or viewpoint of the material. See if it is well written, if the arguments are well supported, and if the author seems to know his or her field. Unless the source is a reference book, you can take the book out of the library and examine it at home. If it is a reference book, you can either photocopy relevant chapters or take notes in the library.

If you decide a source might be helpful in writing your paper, it's time for you to read it carefully, digest it, and take notes on it. These notes will eventually become essential parts of your paper, so it is extremely important that you take them carefully and accurately. By being organized now, you will find it easier to work when it comes time to write the paper.

# What to Read For

When you are reading through sources, it may be difficult for you to determine exactly what you are looking for. This especially holds true in the initial stages of research because you have not yet entirely formulated your thesis or conceived of the overall points in your paper.

It might therefore be helpful to begin by reading a healthy sampling of the sources you have tracked down *before* beginning to take notes. This will enable you to develop a background knowledge of the relevant research concerning your topic. Gaining an understanding of the field, particularly of the kinds of studies that have been conducted, will also help you to fine-tune your thesis. When you have a better idea of what you are looking for, you can then go back to various sources, reread them more carefully, and take notes.

When you are taking notes on a source, the first thing to look for is anything that relates to your general topic. Not all of this will necessarily relate to your thesis, but these notes will help you develop a broad background knowledge. Also, take notes on anything that you find particularly interesting or that sheds light on your topic. You are much better off taking a lot of notes now and throwing out what you don't use later than not taking enough notes and having to return to sources. At the same time, you should not be afraid to return to a source later, when you have a better idea of what your paper will be about and want to look for a relevant point.

# Quoting vs. Paraphrasing

There are two main types of notes derived from secondary source material: quotations and paraphrases.

A *quotation* is a restatement of a passage or a part of a passage from a secondary source presented in the original writer's *exact words*. A *paraphrase*, on the other hand, is a restatement of the ideas in a passage, rephrased in *your own* words.

When you are reading a source and come across a sentence or passage you think is relevant, decide whether or not you want to paraphrase it or quote it. The best method is to paraphrase the larger passages; it is too tedious and time-consuming to copy them down, and they are too lengthy to be included in your paper. If the passage is worded in a particularly interesting or powerful way that you think will stand well on its own in your paper, then you might want to quote it. However, if you're in doubt, you are always better off quoting the source in your notes; you can later paraphrase it from your notes when you write the paper.

If you decide to quote from the source, *copy the line or lines exactly as they appear in the original source, and be certain to put it in quotation marks.* Quoting means you copy it *exactly* as it appears—including any strange spelling or grammatical features.

If something is spelled incorrectly or is grammatically incorrect in the original, you can put the phrase *sic* after the error in brackets to indicate you are aware of the unusual spelling or grammar:

*Gertrude Stein describes one of the women in Three Lives as "a small, spare, german [sic] woman...."*

If you decide to paraphrase the source, *rephrase it completely in your own terms.* Make certain that your paraphrase is an accurate restatement of the main point of the passage.

## Examples of Quotations and Paraphrases

### Source

> Shakespeare's theme in all his history plays is the importance of order and degree, of the disruptive effects of civil strife and rebellion. But as he matured as a dramatist (and *I Henry IV* stands at the beginning of his great period of maturity), he found character to be more interesting than the philosophy or events of history.
>
> (From page 888 of *The Norton Anthology of English Literature,* vol. 1. Ed. M. H. Abrams. 5th ed. New York: Norton, 1986.)

### Quotation from Source in Notes:

*"Shakespeare's theme in all his history plays is the importance of order and degree, of the disruptive effects of civil strife and rebellion. But as he matured as a dramatist (and 1 Henry IV stands at the beginning of his great period of maturity), he found character to be more interesting than the philosophy or events of history."*

Taking Notes 31

Paraphrase of source in notes:

*All of Shakespeare's history plays are concerned with the need to maintain order in the state. However, in later plays, starting with 1 Henry IV, he became interested more in character than historical events and philosophy.*

**Partial Quotation of Source**   If you do not want to copy an entire passage for a quotation, you can use an ellipsis to indicate that material has been omitted. Use three spaced dots to indicate an omission in the middle of a sentence, and four spaced periods to indicate an omission at the end of a sentence:

*"Shakespeare's theme in all his history plays is the importance of order and degree. . . . But as he matured as a dramatist . . . he found character to be more interesting than the philosophy or events of history."*

**Partial Quotation/Partial Paraphrase of Source**   You can also paraphrase part of a passage and quote another part. Be extremely careful when you do this that you put quotation marks around whatever words and phrases you have quoted from the source:

*Shakespeare's history plays are concerned with "the importance of order and degree, of the disruptive effects of civil strife and rebellion." But in his later plays, starting with 1 Henry IV, he "found character to be more interesting than the philosophy or events of history."*

**Using Brackets in Quotations**   If you take a quotation out of context, you may need to clarify part of it, such as indicating to whom certain pronouns refer. You can do this by putting your own terms in brackets in the middle of the quotation. The brackets indicate that you have added or rephrased this part of the quotation. You should only do this for single words and short phrases and only for the purpose of clarity:

*"But as [Shakespeare] matured as a dramatist . . . he found character to be more interesting than the philosophy or events of history."*

# Indirect Quotations and Paraphrases

Occasionally, you may have to quote or paraphrase a part of a source in which that author has quoted or paraphrased someone else. When using indirect sources, you must pay careful attention to documentation (see Chapter VIII on Paper Format). For now, just be careful when you take your notes. If you are quoting, copy down the section exactly as it appears, putting the quotations within the passage in single quotation marks to indicate there is a quotation within the quotation.

For both quotations and paraphrases, be certain to copy down the author's name and the title of the source that your source indirectly mentions. You may have to look carefully for this information, either in the source's bibliography, in previous footnotes, or previous chapters of a book.

# Notes on Primary Texts

Quotations from primary texts are some of the strongest forms of evidence you can include in a paper. If your paper centers upon a primary source or sources—such as works of literature or historical or philosophical essays and documents—you need to take notes from these as well. Just as you do with your secondary sources, you can take notes on your primary texts on note cards (see pg. 34). Then you will easily be able to integrate them into your paper along with the other notes.

# Plagiarism in Notes: A Warning

Plagiarism occurs when a writer uses someone else's ideas or words but does not give the original writer credit and passes off the material as his or her own. Committing plagiarism is regarded as an extremely serious act that, if detected, can have severe consequences. In writing your paper, taking care to avoid committing plagiarism should be your primary concern.

Most people think of plagiarism as when a student copies from or steals another student's paper. Such blatant cases of plagiarism are the most serious and can result in expulsion from school or even legal action.

What most people do not realize, however, is that there are many less blatant cases of plagiarism that may be unintentional on the part of the writer. Writing a research paper differs significantly from other writing assignments: you are not only allowed to use other writers' material but are encouraged to do so. But you must *always give credit where credit is due.* Any time you get an idea or a phrase from another source and do not credit the original source, you are committing plagiarism. Be certain to read Chapter VIII, "Paper Format" for how to credit sources.

There are two points in the paper-writing process at which you must be especially careful so as to avoid accidentally committing plagiarism. One is when you document sources in the body of your paper (discussed at length in Chapter VIII); the other is when you originally take your notes. This is why it is crucial to take very precise notes and keep them organized. Make certain that you always identify the source and page number in your notes.

Be especially careful when you paraphrase or quote from an outside source in your notes. If you paraphrase something, it must be completely rephrased in your own words and then attributed to the source. If a writer coins a particular phrase or describes something in an unusual way and you want to use it, you must enclose it in quotation marks. This even applies to single words, when the author uses them to describe something in an unusual or innovative way, as in the following example:

### Source:

> Milton's epic begins with a rush.
> [From page 1445 of *The Norton Anthology of English Literature*, vol. 1. 5th ed.]

### Plagiarized in Notes:

*Paradise Lost begins with a rush.*

The above note would be considered plagiarism because the word *rush*, an unusual way to describe the beginning of the poem, is not placed in quotation marks.

Once again, the importance of taking careful notes cannot be underestimated. Be *extremely* careful when you take your notes so as to avoid the possibility of inadvertently committing plagiarism.

# The Note Card Method

There are many possible ways to take notes from source materials. Some people keep notes in notebooks or on legal pads; others make photocopies and then highlight parts as they read and make notes in the margins. Many high school writing courses teach students to research term papers using note cards. Teachers might require that their students use this method and turn in their note cards for grading.

The reason teachers encourage students to use note cards is that they are one of the most efficient and organized means of taking notes for a research paper. As with bibliography cards, note cards enable greater flexibility; you can shuffle the cards, organize them in various groupings, and toss out unneeded notes with ease. Writers particularly find using note cards valuable when it comes time to begin writing because it places all the needed information at their fingertips, neatly organized in one convenient place.

It is therefore highly recommended that you use note cards, especially when first learning how to write a research paper.

As you work more as a writer, you will eventually develop a note-taking system that works best for you. To begin, though, try the note cards. You may find it somewhat tedious at first, but the benefits will soon become apparent, and the results will show in your paper. As you did with the bibliography cards, take these notes on index cards. On each card, you will write down one piece of information from a particular source. There is no set format for a note card, as long as you include the necessary information (unless your instructor requires you to do them a certain way, in which case you should follow his or her guidelines).

Before you take notes on any source make certain that you have a complete bibliography card. Because these cards will already have all the bibliographic information from the source, you will not have to keep rewriting it on each note card but can simply cross-reference the cards.

In the top left-hand corner of the card, copy down the last name of the author of the source. If you are using more than one source by a particular author, you should write down the author's last name and a key word or words from the title of that particular source. This will enable you to distinguish between notes taken from different titles. Although unnecessary, you might want to do this on all of your note cards. This will ensure that you do not forget which source the note came from should you eventually use another source by the same author.

In the top right-hand corner, write down the page number of the outside source from which you are taking notes. Keep very careful track of page numbers in your notes. If you are copying down a quotation that begins on one page and ends on the next, mark the exact point in the quotation where the next page begins. If you then only include part of the quotation in your paper, you will then know which page to attribute it to in your documentation.

Use the remaining lines on the card to take down your notes. If you are copying down a quotation, remember to use quotation marks. Also, remember to copy the quotation *exactly* as it appears in the original source and to note any page breaks. If you are paraphrasing, make certain you rephrase the passage completely in your own words. To further ensure that you clearly distinguish between quotations and paraphrases, it is a good idea to write either "QUOTATION" or "PARAPHRASE" at the top of the card in big, bold letters.

Each card should focus upon a single, specific idea. Copying lengthy quotations and paraphrasing large chunks of the source takes away the flexibility that note cards allows you in the first place. Try to confine each card to a single point.

Although it's not necessary, you might want to use the back of the card to make some of your own notes. While you are conducting research, your mind will be at work on the paper, and you will begin to conceive of various points to make in your paper. Unfortunately, these ideas can often get lost in the onslaught of information you are taking in, so you should therefore make certain to write things down. The note cards are the perfect place to do so.

## Sample Note Card

> *Abrams, Supernaturalism*   p.193
> (QUOTATION)
> The "Romantic plot of the circular or spiritual quest" represents an "implicit theodicy; for the journey is a spiritual way through evil and suffering which is justified as a necessary means to a greater good...."

# VI.

# Plan of Attack: The Outline

If you're trying to get somewhere you've never been before without a map, chances are you'll get lost. The same holds true for writing your paper.

Many writers make the mistake of doing research and then plunging headfirst into the writing process. Often, these papers seem aimless, lack focus, fail to make points effectively, and are difficult to read. The truth is, if you do not have a plan, writing the paper will be more difficult. It takes enormous energy to write off the top of your head, and you'll probably wind up staring at a blank sheet of paper not knowing where to begin. As with taking a trip, it's much easier if you know both where you've come from and where you're going.

You therefore need to plot out exactly what you plan to say in your paper *before* you begin writing. The most effective way to do this is by making an outline. An outline is simply a list of the main points you intend to make in your paper, in the approximate order in which you plan to address them.

You're probably thinking to yourself: *When am I going to write this thing already?*

Although doing an outline may seem tedious, it is not a meaningless exercise. It will make the process of writing the paper much easier for you. Everything will be in one place and organized; instead of shuffling through notes and papers, you'll be free to concentrate on writing brilliantly.

The outline will also enable you to plot out a strategy as you order your points to instill them with maximum impact and power. By definition, strategy is something that is planned in advance. When a general plans an attack, he does it before the fight begins, not when he's already feeling the heat of battle and it's too late to make plans. By the same token, strategy cannot develop randomly when you are in the midst of writing. The time to plot out your strategy is before you begin writing—in the outline.

You do not, however, have to wait until you have completed your research to begin designing an outline. You can make a "working outline" while you research. This will help you keep track of all the information you are compiling and ensure that no bright ideas slip through the cracks. Like your working bibliography, the working outline will develop as you conduct research, eventually becoming a final outline. As it is primarily for your own benefit, you can revise the working outline as often as you like. (Occasionally, instructors will require that students submit working outlines, in which case you will have to write one that is a bit more formal than one you would write just for yourself. You can use the same format as for a final outline.)

Before constructing the final outline, you should have a pretty strong sense of what you intend to say in the paper, including several main points you plan on making to prove your argument. These ideas will form naturally out of the research process. Somewhere in the back of your mind you've been thinking about your thesis statement and the paper all along; you've been making connections between different sources and relating them to your own understanding of the material. If you don't have many ideas at this point, you probably need to do more research or maybe even change your thesis. Only when you believe you have enough material for the paper—enough to prove the thesis beyond a shadow of a doubt—will you be ready to make a final outline and then begin writing.

The outline, in effect, is a mirror image of the actual paper. So it is necessary to have an understanding of the structure of a research paper before you design your outline. We will examine the paper structure in the next chapter. Read both this chapter and the next before making your outline.

# Shuffling the Deck:
# Working with the Note Cards

The first step toward creating the final outline is to reexamine your notes. After you feel you've taken enough of them, take all of the cards and skim through them.

Sorting through the note cards is a weeding-out process. As you read through the cards, evaluate how effective their contents might be in your paper, and if the notes are even necessary for your paper. Decide if a note does in fact relate to your thesis; if not, feel free to toss it aside.

The majority of the notes you have taken will probably not apply to your thesis statement, but that's okay. You should have plenty of material left. And by carefully evaluating the notes, you ensure that only the most powerful material remains. You are merely picking the gems out of a substantial lode of raw materials. One of the qualities that separates a good writer from a mediocre one is knowing not only what to put in but what to leave out. **Everything in the paper has to support the thesis statement.** Everything else just adds clutter to your paper, distracting the reader from your argument and thereby detracting from its overall impact.

It might feel painful to throw away material; you may wonder why you made all that effort in the first place. Rest assured that all that note taking has helped make you an expert in your field, and your paper will show it.

As you read through the note cards, begin to group those cards that seem to belong together. You can start by separating them into the most general categories, spreading them out in piles around the room. Try to conceive of a key word or words to describe each category. For example, if you are writing a paper about *"Hamlet and Madness,"* you might have categories such as "The Ghost," "Hamlet and Ophelia," and "Hamlet's Theatricality."

Put the category name on the top of each card in that pile. This way you won't have to worry if the cards become mixed up or further separated.

Since each note card is supposed to focus upon a single idea, you should be able to group the cards into distinct categories. If a card seems to belong in more than one category, place it in the one that seems most applicable (though you may want to note the other categories in which it might be used in case you later decide to move it.)

These categories will be similar to the main sections of your outline and your paper. When you write, you will probably want to narrow down even further, removing cards or even whole categories. For now, however, you have a general sense of the material at your disposal. Your paper is beginning to take shape.

Within each category, you can then subdivide into smaller sections. These subcategories contribute to and help support the various major points in the paper. These notes might eventually become specific paragraphs or parts of paragraphs in your paper.

# Standard Outline Format

The outline simply lists the major points of the essay and, beneath the major points, the subpoints and sub-subpoints that are a part of each. Using Roman numerals, capital letters, lowercase letters, and numbers, the outline orders the various categories so that the smaller subpoints are always listed beneath the more general ones to which they apply. As subpoints become more removed from the major point, they are indented more in the outline. Whenever two points are aligned—meaning that they are indented equally—they carry approximately the same weight in the overall paper.

The major points are listed with a Roman numeral. Subpoints of these major categories are then listed beneath them by capital letter and sub-subpoints beneath them by number. You can continue listing subpoints by using lowercase letters and numbers and letters in parentheses.

This is a sketch of the overall ordering of an outline:

    I. **Major Point One**
        A. **Subpoint of I.**
            1. **Subpoint of A. (sub-subpoint of I.)**
            2. **Subpoint of A. (sub-subpoint of I.)**
        B. **Subpoint of I.**
   II. **Major Point Two**

In the sample above, Roman Numeral I refers to some major point in the paper. Both A and B, indented equally beneath Roman Numeral I, are both subpoints of I. Since A comes first, it is probably a bit more important or extensive than B. Beneath A, there are two subpoints that refer to or support A. By extension, they refer to Roman Numeral I as well.

Here's an example of how an actual outline might look. This one is for part of a paper on "*Hamlet* and Madness":

    I. **Introduction**
   II. **Hamlet as an Actor**
        A. **Hamlet's Theatricality**
            1. **Makes speech to the players**
            2. **Engineers theatrical "scenes"**
                a. **The Mousetrap production**
                b. **Rosencrantz and Guildenstern's death**
        B. **Hamlet "Plays" Mad**
            1. **Plans to put on an "antic disposition"**
            2. **Urges Ophelia, "Get thee to a nunnery."**

Do you see how each subpoint is a subset of the one above it, which is in turn a subset of the one above it?

In general, you can continue adding points and subpoints as long as you like by continuing to indent and change the style of classification (from number to letter, from uppercase to lowercase). Outlines usually follow this general order:

     I.
        A.
            1.
                a.
                    (1)
                        (a)
                        (b)
                    (2)
                b.
            2.
        B.
    II.

Logically, if you are dividing a point into subpoints, you have to divide it into more than one part. In other words, if you list an A there should also be a B.

There are two kinds of formal outlines: the topic outline and the sentence outline. A topic outline lists the various points in phrases, using just a few key words, such as in the above sample outline on *Hamlet*. A topic outline is clean, concise, and to the point, and allows a great degree of freedom and flexibility.

A sentence outline, as its name implies, lists various points using complete, grammatically correct sentences. You will want to use a sentence outline primarily when someone else is to read it, because it makes it easier for the other person to follow your line of thinking. If you are required to submit an outline for your class, you should ask your instructor for guidelines as to the format and style.

If you are making the outline just for yourself, you need not worry about strict formats; do whatever makes the most sense to you. As long as you can distinguish between the major points, subpoints, and sub-subpoints, you can list the various categories however you like.

## Designing Your Outline

After going through your notes, you'll be sitting with several piles of note cards spread out, all made up of the general categories and smaller subcategories within them. Believe it or not, that's your outline. These piles simply become listings of points and subpoints in the outline. The only thing you need to do is decide what order to put the categories in.

The standard research paper is divided into three parts: Introduction, Body, and Conclusion. Roman numeral I on your outline will always be the introduction. The last Roman numeral will always be the conclusion. Underneath the Roman numeral for the introduction, write out your thesis statement, because this is where it will go in the paper. You don't necessarily have to put in anything else right now, unless you have an idea of what you want to say in the introduction.

Everything between the introduction and conclusion is known as the body of the paper. It is here that you will include all the evidence, from your research and your own ideas, that supports the thesis statement. Your general category headings from your note cards will be listed by Roman numerals on the outline. The cards within those categories will then be listed as subpoints of the larger ones, using letters and numbers.

Deciding the order in which to place the categories and subcategories is not that easy; you can't simply throw the cards in the air and list them in whatever order they land. (In the next chapter on Paper Structure, we'll examine some ways of organizing the body of the paper; reading that chapter will help you to organize your outline as well.)

In general, there are two basic organizing principles you need to keep in mind:

**1. Logic.** When organizing the outline, make certain that you order the points in a logical fashion. You want one point to lead to the next, so that the reader will be able to follow your argument without having to fill in gaps that have been left unexplained.

Keeping logic in mind, certain categories will have to follow others and will ultimately order themselves. For example, if you are going to contradict a particular theory, you first need to describe the theory before giving your evidence against it or else it won't make any sense. After reading over the note cards and organizing them into categories, you probably already have some idea which ones will have to be described earlier in the paper in order for later ones to make sense.

There are many ways to organize a paper, but the overall governing organizational principle is logic. For example, if you are writing a historical term paper, it may make the most sense to order your facts chronologically, particularly if you are trying to establish a domino-style momentum to the events. On the other hand, when analyzing a work of literature, it is not necessary to discuss events in the plot in chronological order. In this case, you are analyzing the work as a whole, and you can freely discuss whatever events in the plot relate to your point.

Examine your groupings of note cards and see if you can determine which ones must logically go together or follow one another. You probably won't have the entire outline completed, and you may not know yet where to place certain categories. However, you will have gotten a start on ordering your paper.

**2. Strategy.** Although the most important factor to consider is that the order makes logical sense, you also want to organize your points so that they will be especially powerful in building your case. Thus, you need to decide on a strategy.

Before lawyers go to court, they carefully prepare how they intend to present their evidence, the order in which they plan to call up witnesses, and what line of questioning they will follow. They do all of this with a plan in mind that will help their case. For example, there's a reason why the surprise witness is always called in last, creating a hush over the spectators. Having a surprise witness appear last is a strategic decision that has great dramatic impact. In writing your paper, you need to think along similar crafty, strategic lines.

Evaluate your different pieces of evidence. Some no doubt will be more powerful than others; these are your star witnesses. With this in mind, consider how to order these pieces of evidence so that they make the most persuasive argument and pack the most punch. Strategically, you may want to build up to your strongest points so as to leave your reader with these ideas foremost in mind and absolutely convinced of your argument. But at the same time, you won't want to start with your weakest points and give the reader a lukewarm first impression.

Strategy is a personal decision. Each writer will have his or her own favorite strategic devices, and each paper will have its own strategic method behind it. You need to consider the overall effect you want to create in the paper and the way you want to go about achieving it.

# Fine-Tuning the Outline

When trying to arrange your various groupings of note cards into an order for the outline, it may be easier to begin by organizing the smaller subcategories within each category. As all of these subcategories are closely related to one another, logic patterns will probably be more evident. Organizing the larger categories—your main points of the paper—is a bit more difficult, because this is where you have a lot more choice and will need to think strategically.

Remember, the outline is not written in stone. When you are in the rhythm of writing the paper, you may find that a certain point works much better in a different place than you had originally planned. That's okay. You can veer from the path a bit, but you'll still be heading in the same direction that you plotted out beforehand.

Try to make the outline as detailed as possible. The more specific the details in the outline, the easier it will be to write your paper. Beneath the categories on the outline, you can list various sources (and even page numbers of sources) that you plan to discuss in relation to the category. You might even write out specific quotations you intend to introduce at that point in the paper.

Take the time to plan everything now. You won't regret it later. and you won't get "lost" in the midst of writing.

# VII.

# Paper Structure

The structure of most standard term papers is similar to a court proceeding. In a trial, the lawyer first makes opening remarks, briefly stating for the judge or jury the exact status of his or her case (such as how the client pleads) and how, through the course of the proceedings, he or she intends to prove it. Next, the lawyer spends the bulk of the legal proceeding carefully and methodically presenting evidence that supports the case. Finally, when finished presenting evidence, the lawyer will give a summation, quickly recapping the main points that have proven the case.

A standard paper is structured in much the same way as a legal proceeding, with three distinct parts that roughly correspond to the parts of a trial and fulfill the same purpose. They're called the **introduction**, the **body**, and the **conclusion**.

# The Introduction

Like the lawyer's opening statement, the introduction of the paper is where you lay out your argument for the judge—your instructor. Most introductions will be only one paragraph, although in bigger projects (more than twenty pages, such as a master's thesis or dissertation) it might be somewhat longer. As in a trial, you do not want to spend the bulk of the proceeding just setting up your argument; you want to spend it actually arguing. By being succinct, the introduction will be more to the point and have much more impact.

You want the introduction to seduce your reader into your argument right from the beginning. It's somewhat like a movie preview; you're going to give your audience a short taste of what's to come, but not the whole story. You want your reader to be enticed, immediately interested in what you have to say, and curious as to how you are going to go about saying it. The introduction should grab the reader, pull him or her into the body of the paper.

Because it summarizes the gist of your argument, your thesis statement will naturally be an important part of the introduction. But it can't be an introduction on its own. In most cases, the thesis statement will be only one sentence, certainly too short to make an impressive introduction. Moreover, as we have seen, a thesis statement is very specific and often represents a different or unusual view of the material. If you simply write out your thesis statement at the top of the paper without elaborating on it, you are probably going to confuse or even annoy the reader. You therefore need to set the stage before introducing the thesis to your reader.

The standard form of the introduction is structured to set up the thesis statement. The last sentence of the introduction will be the thesis statement, enabling you to use the entire paragraph to set the stage. The introductory paragraph is thus a kind of introduction to your thesis statement, beginning in a general manner and slowly easing the reader into your argument. You want the bulk of the introduction to establish the general arena from which your thesis emerges and within which you will be presenting your argument in the paper.

The first sentence of the introduction—the first sentence of your entire paper—is your reader's first taste of the topic and your point of view. Make certain that you make a good first impression. The sentence should be well written, interesting, and, most important, give the reader some idea what the paper is going to be about.

The rest of the introduction bridges together this first general statement and the thesis statement. After your opening line, each subsequent sentence will be literally and figuratively one step closer to the thesis statement. By the time the reader comes to your thesis statement, he or she should have a strong sense of the kind of paper this is going to be, what issues and topics it will be addressing, and the writer's take on them.

Before writing the introduction, you only needed an idea of what your thesis statement would say. Now, you will have to decide upon the exact wording. When you write the thesis statement in your introduction, it is the first and possibly the only place in which you will spell it out for your reader. You therefore need to be extremely careful about the wording of your thesis statement in the introduction. You want to phrase it so that it will not be at all ambiguous. It does not have to be fancy, flashy, or wordy; the power of the idea should be enough to impress your reader.

Like the thesis statement, the introduction should come from you. In general, this is not the place to begin introducing your secondary sources. The secondary sources, as we will see, will be presented in the body of the paper to support whatever argument you initially set up in the introduction. It would not make sense to present evidence without first stating what argument you are trying to make. Moreover, you want the reader to be immediately impressed by the power of your own voice, the depth of your understanding of the topic, and the strength of your own ideas.

This is an example of a standard, straightforward introduction:

<u>In Shakespeare's plays, madness and tragedy seem to go hand in hand.</u> All of his great tragic figures, including Macbeth and Lady Macbeth, Othello, Hamlet, and King Lear, grapple with madness in some form or other. To a large extent, their insanity illuminates aspects of their character, as Shakespeare uses it to convey the personal torment and anguish that these characters experience in the wake of their tragic circumstances. However, Shakespeare not only uses insanity to point out a tragic character's personal torment but also to convey his or her alienation from the larger social structure.

*Begins with Broad, General Statement*

↓

*Becomes More Specific*

*Thesis Statement*

The above introduction begins with a generalized statement that lets the reader know the topic: in this case, madness in Shakespeare's tragedies. It then narrows down to the thesis statement, laying out a specific point of view on the topic.

There are several variations on this standard format. Although we said that the introduction is generally not the place in which to introduce secondary sources, one effective format does draw on the research you have conducted. In this variation of the standard introduction, you begin by summarizing a trend in the critical material and research on your subject. You then set up how your thesis either conforms to or differs from this body of material.

When you write this kind of introduction, you do not specify individual sources but instead write a general summation of a body of sources. Just make certain that your summation is accurate, that it does in fact summarize a substantial portion of the secondary material. (To ensure that you do not leave yourself open to attack on this point, you should include a bibliographic note—a footnote at the bottom of the page listing several secondary sources that support your statement.)

*Notes a Critical Trend Becomes More Specific* ⬇

*Thesis Statement*

<u>Many critics, writing in the wake of Freud, have primarily addressed the question of Hamlet's sanity.</u> A body of scholarly material is devoted to answering the question of whether or not Hamlet, in playing mad, actually goes mad. However, by focusing all discussion of the play on Hamlet's individual psyche, critics have ignored the larger social setting that Shakespeare so carefully establishes. The social setting and Hamlet's psyche are intricately interwoven, as Shakespeare uses madness to indicate Hamlet's alienated status within the larger society of the play.

This introduction is much more centered on the scholarly discussion of the play. The first sentence not only lets the reader know that this will be a paper about *Hamlet* and madness but says it will be a highly analytical paper, centered in criticism and research. The writer begins by summarizing a critical trend, without going into too much specific detail about it. (A bibliographical note would list several essays that support this assertion.) After presenting this summation of a critical trend, the writer then discusses what he or she sees as the problem with this viewpoint and finally presents the thesis statement, which counters it.

Similarly, if your entire argument hinges upon some influential theory, book, essay, or article, or the ideas of a particular researcher or critic, then you will probably want to mention that particular source in your introduction. However, you must still follow the same conventions of a standard introduction. The influential source you describe serves as the general arena out of which your thesis statement emerges. In the introduction, you describe the gist of this particular secondary source *in general terms,* and then establish how your argument either agrees with or differs from it. You will elaborate on the specifics of the source later in your paper.

## Tips on Writing an Introduction

As these examples demonstrate, there are many different ways to approach the introduction. Be aware, however, that how you approach your topic in the introduction sets up certain expectations for your reader about the rest of the paper. Try to take into consideration the effect you want to produce in the paper as a whole and how you can set it up in the introduction. Do you want to be descriptive, analytical, or critical? Do you want to describe or challenge a particular trend or theory? Do you want to challenge or intrigue the reader? The tone and style of the language you use will help you to produce the desired effect.

At first, you may want to write very standard introductions. As you become more comfortable with writing papers, you will feel more confident being creative and even daring in the introduction. No matter how you write the introduction, *make certain that it establishes the paper's topic and that it clearly presents the thesis.*

The introduction should feature some of the strongest writing in your paper. This means it will take somewhat more thought and effort. Just because it comes first, however, does not mean that you necessarily have to write it first. Many writers try to begin at the beginning and, faced with the pressure of writing a brilliant introduction, find themselves frozen. As long as you have a thesis statement, you can skip the introduction for now and begin writing the rest of the paper. After designing your outline, you're probably more than ready to start writing the body of the paper, so it will be an easier place to begin. Once you have written a part or even all of the body, you will have a better idea of what you want to say in your introduction. You can then go back to the beginning.

# The Body

The body formulates the bulk of your paper; it's where you will at last argue your case in detail. After having conducted research and given your topic great thought, you should have several points you want to make to prove your thesis. In the body, you will present these ideas.

The most important thing to keep in mind is that *every bit of information you include in the body should relate to the thesis, and you must spell out exactly how it does.* Remember, the reader cannot see inside your head. You must therefore explain all your points very carefully, making it crystal clear for the reader what they mean and how they tie into and support your overall argument.

## The Evidence: Bringing in the Sources

Merely listing your ideas is not enough to prove your thesis conclusively. This is why you need to bring in supporting evidence from your primary and secondary sources, because they lend greater credence to your ideas. This does not mean, however, that these outside sources replace your own ideas. You are bringing them in to support your ideas, not to overwhelm them.

Each time you quote or paraphrase from an outside source, you need to include a citation that documents the source's origin. This is done according to a standard format, so it will be clear to anyone reading your paper what ideas come from outside sources. Make certain you read the next chapter on Paper Format, which discusses how to cite outside sources.

If your paper is centered upon some primary source—meaning that you are mainly analyzing a particular work or works—it is extremely important that you draw upon the primary source extensively in your paper. Facts drawn directly from the primary source are the strongest kinds of evidence you have at your disposal. As they have not been translated through another person's eyes, they are a much more valid—and therefore potent—form of evidence. You should try to quote from a primary source often and in detail. Make certain, though, to cite the source with a page number.

You will also include material drawn from your secondary sources. You must demonstrate your knowledge of the research that has been conducted by various experts in the field. These established researchers and writers can help lend support to your interpretation of the text. These sources are not irrefutable, however, and you may counter what they say, as long as you have strong evidence supporting your view.

## Overall Direction of the Body

The body should not randomly bring up points and then drop them in a haphazard fashion. Instead, it should have an overall direction, with the various points building on one another and propelling the paper forward. This is where strategic planning comes into play, which you can try to map out in your outline.

There are various ways to plot out the overall arc of the paper's body, and you should consider one that best serves your purposes. One common way to organize the body is to begin your discussion in broad, general terms, laying a solid groundwork for more sophisticated points to come. After establishing the main, less refutable points, your discussion can then become progressively more specific and complex. It is like building a house: you first lay out a sturdy foundation and then move on to the more intricate frame.

Another approach is to establish various specific points in the beginning stages of the paper and then tie them into broader, more theoretical schemes in the latter parts.

These are only two common means of organizing the overall arc of the body, but there are many others, and you may find one more suitable to you. Your primary concern should be that the paper flows smoothly, with one idea logically leading to the next. If you organize your paper with this in mind, the body will have a momentum that emerges on its own.

## Ways of Introducing Material

Within the overall arc of the body, there are many ways to introduce and discuss material. Alternating the ways you present your ideas and evidence adds variety to the paper, making it more interesting to read.

Among the many techniques of presenting material you may use, the following are some you can use in any combination:

**1. Description:** This kind of writing features very detailed, highly descriptive language that essentially recreates an object, work, or event in words but without making any kind of critical evaluation.

Certain papers, sometimes called descriptive papers, are almost entirely devoted to description. All papers, however, will have parts in which the writer describes something. For example, if you were to write a paper about a play, such as *Hamlet,* you might choose to describe certain scenes that support your thesis. Similarly, if you were writing a paper on the Civil War, you might include a paragraph in which you describe various modes of combat during the war. These passages help make the paper more colorful, dramatic, and interesting.

However, even when you are describing something in your paper, you still must make certain it relates to the thesis and that your reader will see the connection. You cannot randomly describe things without making the connection clear; this will distract the reader from your argument.

There is an important distinction between description and summary. Description, in elaborating upon a particular work or object, enhances the reader's view of it, and thereby lends additional support to your argument. You use it to highlight a particular side or viewpoint of the work or object. Summarization, on the other hand, is almost always unnecessary in a paper; your reader is probably already familiar with the material and, if not, can certainly find out about it for him or herself.

For example, if you are writing for an English teacher, you need not summarize the plot of *Hamlet;* you can assume the teacher already knows it. You might, though, want to describe a specific scene in order to highlight a particular aspect of it that relates to your argument. If you are discussing the question of Hamlet's sanity, for example, you might describe the scene in which he confronts Polonius as a means of establishing how Hamlet behaves in various situations.

As this example indicates, most descriptive passages work best together with some form of evaluation or analysis that puts the description into perspective and relates it to the overall argument.

You should be careful not to use too many descriptive passages (unless, of course, your assignment is to write a descriptive paper). Description may help make your argument more effective, but it won't prove your argument on its own. You do not want to tie up the body of the paper with descriptions when you should instead be discussing your research and your ideas that will prove your argument. You can describe something in anywhere from a few words to a paragraph. If it takes longer than a paragraph, chances are it is becoming too extensive and is not all that necessary.

In short, *do not include a description unless it will add fuel to your fire.*

**2. Presentation and Definition:** Closely related to description, the presentation or definition of material is another means of including information in the paper. You introduce and define, usually in one or two lines, a particular source or piece of information, without necessarily elaborating upon it. For example, if you are writing a paper about the Civil War, you might include one paragraph in which you present the various perspectives from which the war has been analyzed.

**3. Critical Argument, Evaluation, and Analysis:** Most writing in research papers will be of this type, in which you not only introduce material but proceed to evaluate it from a critical perspective. You do so to establish the information as valid and relevant to your argument or, if it contradicts your argument, to counter it.

All writing is a form of interpretation and therefore open to criticism and evaluation from differing perspectives. When you write your paper, you want to evaluate the material for your reader in such a way that it highlights how it supports your argument. You approach the source material from the perspective of an expert, evaluating it with the benefit of your substantial background knowledge and intimate understanding attained in the process of doing the research. If you do this in a convincing manner, your reader will not question your interpretation or the validity of your argument. In short, you want your reader to buy into your argument without question.

You especially will want to approach primary sources—those texts that are the focus of the paper—in a critical fashion. The essence of most papers is the writer's particular interpretation of some primary source or sources. Draw out the parts of the primary source that agree with your interpretation and criticize or argue against those that disagree.

At the same time, you want to approach your secondary sources in a critical fashion. As you were taking notes, you began evaluating the various sources and determining their validity and the extent to which they might support your argument. Now when you introduce information from these secondary sources in the body of the paper, you can indicate to the reader your critical evaluation of them. For example, you may mention certain theories, studies, or interpretations with which you disagree. You can then proceed to describe why you disagree with these views, using other sources to prove your point. (These kinds of arguments are often made in footnotes; see the next chapter on Paper Format.)

Much of the body might also be devoted to analyzing a specific passage, during which you either quote or paraphrase an entire passage, and then discuss and interpret it in a critical fashion. When you analyze material, always try to do so in detail, referring to specific aspects of it.

**4. Compare/Contrast:** This is a particular type of critical argument that can be especially powerful in helping you prove your case. Very simply, you introduce several pieces of information together (primary or secondary sources or excerpts from them) and evaluate them against each other. You then indicate which ideas or sources are stronger than others and submit these principles in support of your thesis.

**5. Differing Points of View:** This is another means of critical argument, but it is also extremely effective. You introduce one mode of interpretation—for example, a particular theory or study—and then hypothesize in the paper how this interpretation might change if approached from a different point of view.

Example:

**Many critics have argued that Hamlet is a play about a tormented individual. However, it might also be thought of as a play about a tormented society.**

You can then discuss how this different perspective sheds new light on the topic and use it in support of your overall argument.

**6. Personal Response:** This is a kind of writing in which the writer expresses intimate thoughts, feelings, and reactions about a particular subject or brings in personal experiences to reflect on the subject. Of course, all writing is in some form or another a writer's personal response. But most papers are written from an objective standpoint, meaning that the writer is somewhat removed from the material and lets the information and sources stand on their own. In a personal response, the writer is an active presence, and the reader is consciously aware of the writer's voice. This is primarily achieved through the use of first person narrative ("I think," "I feel," etc.)

An instructor will sometimes assign students to write personal responses, but traditionally this kind of writing has been frowned upon in the research paper. However, many institutions are now questioning the validity of this belief and are encouraging students to incorporate personal narrative into their papers. You should not include personal response in your research paper unless your instructor has indicated it is acceptable. When personal response is used, the same rule applies as when you introduce other sources: do so only to the extent that it relates to your thesis, and be certain to spell out exactly how it does.

# Other Tips and Guidelines for Writing the Body

There are many ways to present material and make your points in the body, and they need not be distinguished from one another or labeled as they are above. You already know all the ways to make a convincing argument. Whenever you try to convince someone of your viewpoint in conversation, you make use of the same techniques that you would on paper.

As you concentrate upon ways to prove your thesis, you should naturally be able to come up with convincing arguments. The example of a lawyer arguing a case in court is stressed here because a lawyer's arguments are made orally and therefore seem somewhat less restricted than written arguments. But both written and oral arguments follow the same principles of logic.

It may help you to "talk" through your ideas in your head or even out loud. If you were to try to explain your thesis to a friend, what would you say? How would you describe or introduce the source material to convince your friend? You may actually want to talk through your paper with a friend. Be conscious of how you phrase things, the kinds of arguments you make, and the logic behind them. Whatever you say can be written down.

Chapter IX, "Write Stuff: The Mechanics of Good Writing," includes tips that will help you in your writing of the body. In general, though, keep these guidelines in mind:

**1. Get it all down on paper:** You are so closely tied to your ideas that you can understand them without confusion. Because it all makes perfect sense to you, you may think you have fully explained a point or idea, when in fact you have merely mentioned it on paper. Your reader, of course, can't see into your mind. You have to get the entire idea out on paper and make certain it is clear to an outsider who does not have your insider's view of your own thoughts.

**2. Relates to thesis:** Everything in the body should relate to the thesis statement. If it doesn't, get rid of it; it's only clouding up your argument and detracting from its power. You should also make certain that the connections between the various pieces of information and your thesis are clear to the reader. You may have to spell it out directly.

**3. Smooth flow:** You don't want the paper to be choppy and difficult to read. Instead, one idea should flow smoothly into the next, as you guide your reader through your argument. If this is not the case, you may have to reorder parts of the body.

## The Conclusion

The paper begins with an introduction in which you make a claim—your thesis statement—and a promise to prove your case to your reader. The body of the paper is then spent presenting evidence to achieve this goal. Ultimately, all of this evidence leads right back to the thesis statement, which is now seen from a very different perspective than that found in the introduction.

After reading the body and all the evidence you have presented, the reader should now view your thesis statement not as conjecture but as proven fact. And that's exactly what you are going to tell the reader in your conclusion. Although it is never couched in these explicit terms, all conclusions have the same underlying meaning and say essentially the same thing: I have successfully proven what I said I was going to in my introduction.

The conclusion is therefore a kind of mirror image of your introduction—but one that stresses the fact that the thesis has now been proven. Like the introduction, the conclusion for most term papers need only be one paragraph (unless they are particularly long papers of more than fifteen pages). Also similar to the introduction, the conclusion should come from you and be primarily dominated by your voice and ideas. This is not a place to quote or paraphrase extensively from secondary sources.

While the introduction is the first taste of your paper, your conclusion is the last. You want to end with a bang, with some of your most powerful writing, leaving the reader impressed with your expertise and absolutely convinced of the validity of your argument.

The conclusion should therefore again include the thesis statement in some form or other but affirm that it has been conclusively proven. The standard way to accomplish this, one that many instructors advise their students to use, is to invert the structure of the introduction. You begin by restating the thesis statement, reworded a bit to emphasize that it is now proven, and then expand upon it until you end with a broad, general statement. As in a lawyer's closing summation, you should also try to recap some of the major points you have made in your paper that have helped establish your argument.

This is an example of a standard conclusion for the paper on "Madness in Shakespeare." Compare it to the Sample Introduction above from the same paper:

Shakespeare's tragic figures, then, are removed from the larger societies he depicts in the plays, and he dramatically emphasizes this alienation, as we have seen, through madness. The madness that so many of his tragic figures display is not only the result of their tragic circumstances, but, in a larger sense, symptomatic of it. Shakespeare therefore seems to use madness for a twofold purpose: to indicate something about the nature of the tragic character and to establish something about the individual's role in society.

*Restates (Affirms) Thesis*

*Makes General Conclusion*

This is a standard form of a conclusion. As with the introduction, there are many other ways to approach it. Many writers choose to introduce some new point or question in the conclusion that emerges from the thesis. After establishing the validity of the thesis, they then address its consequences or implications.

Depending on the flexibility and freedom your instructor allows you, you can try to be bold and creative in the conclusion, just as you may in the introduction. However, the same rule applies: *the conclusion must bring the paper to a close and affirm that the thesis has been proven.*

# A Final Word on Structure

The three-part paper structure we have examined here is one found in most term papers. However, it is not a hard and fast law that this format be used. As you read academic books and articles, you will find that some writers follow it and others do not. Many academic institutions are currently questioning the relevance for teaching this standard structure.

Learning about this structure is valuable, however, because it is particularly effective. It ensures that the paper remains focused upon a main idea (the thesis statement), and that it is presented in a straightforward and logical fashion. Understanding and following this structure will probably help you write powerful and persuasive papers, especially when you are first learning how to write. Once you are familiar with and comfortable writing the standard structure, you will get a sense of how you might stray from it but still write strong and compelling papers.

# VIII.

# Paper Format: Documentation, Quotations, and the Bibliography/ Works Cited

Integrating the notes from the primary and secondary sources with your own ideas and presenting it in one neat package can be a logistical nightmare. For this reason, standard formats have been designed that dictate exactly how information should be documented in the paper.

Imagine how difficult it would be to read a paper if each time outside source information was introduced it was in an arbitrary and random fashion: sometimes with the author's last name, sometimes with page numbers, sometimes with the color of the book cover. The paper would literally be a mess, with no way to identify the origin of outside information and almost no way to read straight through. That's why following a standard format is crucial.

A standard format provides consistency within the paper, ensuring that each time the writer introduces an outside source, it is done so in the same way, with all the necessary documentation. It also provides consistency from one paper to the next, so that any reader might pick up any paper and understand it. Most important, it protects the writer from charges of plagiarism, because all outside sources are clearly and consistently credited.

Different formats have come into popular use in the academic world at different times. Currently, the standard format required by most institutions and academic journals is the one that has been developed by the Modern Language Association (MLA).[1] The MLA publishes a handbook that outlines the various aspects of its format for the research paper.

Although we will be highlighting the basics of the MLA format in this chapter, it is highly recommended that you purchase or consult the MLA handbook for yourself; it includes more specific and detailed guidelines.

## Documenting Sources

As we discussed in Chapter V, "Taking Notes," each time you introduce information from an outside source into your paper you must document *exactly* where it came from. You need to do this for everything in your paper that comes from some source other than your own head—whether it be a quotation, paraphrase, or even an idea or theory. In other words, *you must always give credit where credit is due*. If you do not, you are committing plagiarism.

The MLA format dictates the standard way to document sources in your paper. Everything you introduce in your paper from an outside source is documented in two places:

**1. In the text of the paper:** For each piece of information you include from an outside source you must indicate its origin in the text of the paper. Ordinarily this is done using a *parenthetical reference,* an abbreviated documentation—usually the author's last name or the source's title—that appears in the text in parentheses and indicates which source the information came from and exactly where in the source it was found.

**2. In the list of Works Cited:** At the end of the paper, you will include your final bibliography, also called *Works Cited*. The citations in the Works Cited are not abbreviated and list complete publication information about each source.

All of the abbreviated citations within the text of the paper must correspond to a listing in the Works Cited.

---

[1]Note: There are some older formats and styles of documentation, such as the traditional footnote style and the number-date system. Ask your instructor what format to use. If it is other than the MLA format, go to the library and check out a handbook or guide for that format.

For example, look at the following sentence from the body of a paper:

**Buck Mulligan makes his first appearance "bearing a bowl of lather on which a mirror and a razor lay crossed" (Joyce 3).**

The information in parentheses indicates where the quotation comes from: page 3 of some work by someone named Joyce. The Works Cited will then have the following corresponding citation:

**Joyce, James.** *Ulysses.* **New York: Vintage Books, 1986.**

The reader will then know that the quotation comes from page 3 of James Joyce's *Ulysses*.

## Documentation in the Text of the Paper

Within the text of the paper, you have to document all information that comes from outside sources—quotations, paraphrases, and even ideas.

However, you do not need to document hard facts and statements of common knowledge that are not affiliated with a particular source. For example, "The Declaration of Independence was signed on July 4, 1776" or "*Romeo and Juliet* is Shakespeare's tragedy about two young lovers and their feuding families" make factual statements that are self-evident. These kinds of statements need not be documented.

However, you always need to document direct quotations, even if the quotation makes a general, factual statement. If the sentences above had come directly from another source, they would then need to be placed in quotation marks and documented to the source, even though they make factual statements.

*When in doubt, you should always document a piece of information.*

## Parenthetical References

The simplest way to document a source in the body of the paper is to use the parenthetical reference just described. *A parenthetical reference must always correspond to a citation in the Works Cited.*

The most common type of parenthetical reference will list the author's last name and the page number or numbers, as in the following example:

**The Romantic writers shared a common concern with particular problems afflicting humanity and a distinct way of trying to resolve them (Abrams 12).**

In the above sentence, the information in parentheses indicates that the information about Romantic writers comes from page 12 of a source by Abrams. By consulting the Works Cited, the reader could then find the full citation for the source:

**Abrams, M.H.** *Natural Supernaturalism: Tradition and Revolution in Romantic Literature.* **New York: Norton, 1971.**

# Placement of Parenthetical References

A parenthetical reference should always be placed within the text of your paper immediately following the information it documents but without disrupting the flow of the sentence. It can come either at the end of the sentence...

**Many of the Romantic poets viewed the French Revolution as foreshadowing the apocalypse (Abrams 64).**

...or at a natural pause in the sentence, such as after an independent clause:

**Many of the Romantic poets viewed the French Revolution as foreshadowing the apocalypse (Abrams 64), which becomes evident in the tone of Shelley's works.**

But it should always be placed as close to the information it documents as possible:

**Many of the Romantic poets viewed the French Revolution as foreshadowing the apocalypse (Abrams 64), and their works often described feelings of both hope and dejection (Abrams 442).**

The reference should always precede the punctuation (the period or comma) that ends the clause or sentence. If it follows a quotation, it is placed outside the quotation marks but before the final period or comma:

**"In many important philosophers and poets, Romantic thinking and imagination remained apocalyptic thinking and imagination, though with varied changes in explicit content" (Abrams 65).**

If the quotation ends with an ellipsis, the parenthetical reference still goes outside the quotation marks but before the final period:

**"In many important philosophers and poets, Romantic thinking and imagination remained apocalyptic thinking and imagination..." (Abrams 65).**

Similarly, a question mark or exclamation point that comes at the end of a quotation will remain inside the quotation marks, and the parenthetical reference will be placed outside the quotation marks, followed by a period:

**Jane confronts Rochester, "Why did you take such pains to make me believe you wished to marry Miss Ingram?" (Bronte 230).**

However, if the question mark is not a part of the quotation but a part of the sentence, it will follow the parenthetical reference:

**One may well wonder, why does Rochester refer to Jane as his "second self" (Bronte 223)?**

## Variations of Parenthetical References

The information you put in the parenthetical reference depends upon the sources listed in the Works Cited. You should therefore have a working bibliography on hand so that you can see what sources you are going to be using. It will also depend on how much information about the source is included in the text of the paper (see section below on Striving for Clarity).

In most cases, you can simply write the author's last name (or whatever name the source is listed by in the Works Cited, such as the translator or editor) and the page number, as in the examples above. However, there are several special cases that require additional or different information:

• **More than one author with the same last name:** If there is more than one author with the same last name in your list of Works Cited, you can distinguish between the authors in the parenthetical references by using both the last name and each author's first initial or first name:

**"Mr. Rochester was not to me what he had been; for he was not what I had thought him" (Charlotte Bronte 260).**

**"Wuthering Heights is the name of Mr. Heathcliff's dwelling" (Emily Bronte 14).**

• **Work cited by title only:** Some works may not have a published author, such as anonymous works and certain reference guides. These works are listed in the Works Cited alphabetically according to the first word in the title (most others are listed in alphabetical order by author's last name). In the parenthetical reference, you then use the title in place of the author's last name:

**Grendel's mother attacks the hall while the men sleep (*Beowulf* 50).**

However, if the title is long (more than two words), you can abbreviate it, using one or two key words. You should use the first significant word(s) in the title so that the reader can easily find it in the list of Works Cited:

**His pride hurt, Arthur challenges the Green Knight (*Sir Gawain* 277–78).**

In the above reference, *Sir Gawain and the Green Knight* has been abbreviated to *Sir Gawain*.

When you list a work's title in a parenthetical reference, you should use the correct punctuation, either underlining or placing the title in quotation marks (see section on Title Format below).

- **More than one work by the same author:** Sometimes you will use several sources all written by the same author. You will need to distinguish between the sources in the parenthetical references so that the reader will know from which particular source in the list of Works Cited the information is derived. You do this by placing a comma after the author's name and then writing the title of the source:

> **Wordsworth translates Milton's imagery "from a supernatural to a natural frame of reference..." (Abrams, *Natural Supernaturalism* 23).**

> **The Romantic writers were "preoccupied with the fact and idea of revolution" (Abrams, *Norton Anthology* 5).**

If the title is long (more than two or three words), you can use an abbreviated version of the title, writing one or two key words from the title. In the above reference, for example, *The Norton Anthology of English Literature, Volume 2* is abbreviated as *Norton Anthology*. The reader can consult the Works Cited listing to find the full title.

- **More than one author of a source:** Some sources are written by several authors. If a source is listed in the Works Cited with two or three authors, you should list all their last names, separated by commas, in the parenthetical reference. If the work has more than three authors, you should list them in the same way you chose to do so in the Works Cited: either write out all the authors' names or only the first author's name followed by the abbreviation *et al.*

- **More than one relevant source:** Sometimes several sources will pertain to a single piece of information in the paper. If you need to cite more than one source in the parenthetical reference, use the normal format for each one, and separate them with a semicolon, within the same parentheses:

> **The portrait of Camelot presented at the beginning of *Sir Gawain and the Green Knight* is of a younger, more innocent Camelot (Spearing, *Gawain-Poet* 181; Hunt 3).**

As you want to avoid long parenthetical references that will obstruct the reader, you should cite only two or three sources within a parenthetical reference. To cite more than three sources, you can use a footnote or endnote (see section on Bibliographic Notes below).

- **Indirect citations:** The MLA instructs that you should always try to take material from the original source. Occasionally, however, you will want to quote or paraphrase material from the source you are using that has been taken from somewhere else. When you do this, put the abbreviation *qtd. in* (quoted in) before the citation in the parenthetical reference:

**William Wordsworth calls *The Prelude*, "the poem on the growth of my own mind" (qtd. in *Norton Anthology* 227).**

## Citing Locations Within Sources

In the parenthetical reference, you not only identify the original source of the information included in the text, but you identify the exact location of that information within the source. You can usually do this by putting the page number(s) following the author and/or title. When citing a range of numbers, give the second number in full for all numbers below 100. For numbers above 100, abbreviate the second number to the last two digits. Never use the abbreviation "*p.*" or "*pp.*"; simply skip a space and write the page number(s):

**(Abrams 62)**
**(Bronte, *Jane Eyre* 20–25)**

You do not need to list page numbers for articles that are only one-page long.

In certain instances, you may need to include additional or more specific information than page numbers:

### Multivolume Works

If your Works Cited list includes more than one volume of a particular source, you need to indicate the specific volume in the parenthetical reference. You can do this by writing the volume number, followed by a colon and the page numbers. You do not need to write "volume" or "vol.":

**(*Norton Anthology* 2: 54–55)**

If you are only using one volume of a series, you do not need to include the volume number in the parenthetical reference; it will appear in the Works Cited.

### Literary Works

**Prose:** The MLA recommends that when you cite prose literary works, you include information in addition to page numbers, such as a chapter or scene number. Although not required, it is highly recommended you do this because it enables a reader to find the quotation in editions other than the one you might be using.

List the page number first, followed by a semicolon and whatever additional information you wish to include, abbreviating words such as *chapter* and *scene*.

**Huck decides, "It warn't no use for me to try to learn to do right..." (76; ch. 16).**

**Verse:** When citing verse plays and poems, do not use page numbers at all. For poems, cite according to line numbers:

> **Keats addresses the urn, "Thou still unravish'd bride of quietness, / Thou foster-child of silence and slow time..." ("Grecian Urn" 1–2).**

You should also indicate if there are larger divisions, such as cantos or parts of the poem, listing the larger division first, followed by a period and then the line numbers:

> **Milton describes Adam and Eve, "in their looks divine, / The image of their glorious Maker..." (*Paradise Lost* 4.291–92).**

In the above parenthetical reference, the 4 refers to Book 4, and the 291–92 to the line numbers within Book 4.

The MLA recommends that the first time you cite from a poem, you write out the word *line* or *lines* to establish that the citation refers to line numbers. Once this is established, you list only the line numbers.

**Verse Drama:** You should cite lines from verse plays by indicating act, scene, and line numbers and separating them with periods. The MLA recommends using Arabic as opposed to Roman numerals. However, many writers still prefer Roman numerals for act and scene divisions to avoid confusion:

> **"The play's the thing / Wherein I'll catch the conscience of the King" (*Hamlet* 2.2.616–17) or (*Hamlet* II.ii.616–17).**

## Striving for Clarity; Eliminating Repetition

The information about the source that you include in the parenthetical references will depend not only on the Works Cited list but on how much information about the source is included in the text of the paper.

The purpose of using parenthetical references is to indicate the origin of a piece of information in the paper clearly and without tying up the paper and distracting the reader. If the text of your paper makes it obvious where a particular piece of information comes from, you need not repeat it in the parenthetical reference because it is redundant. You still have to include a parenthetical reference detailing the location within the source, such as the page number:

> **Abrams argues that many Romantic poets viewed the French Revolution as foreshadowing the apocalypse (64).**

In the above example, the author's name is clearly identified in the text. It is not necessary to also include it in the parentheses, but the page number still must be included.

In the following example, the parenthetical references must also include additional information about titles:

**In one of his comedies, Shakespeare writes, "all the world's a stage / And all the men and women merely players" (*As You Like It* 2.7.139–40). However, this theatrical motif also plays a part in the tragedies, such as when one tragic figure exclaims, "Life's but a walking shadow, a poor player, / That struts and frets his hour upon the stage, / And then is heard no more" (*Macbeth* 5.5.24–26).**

The content of the above paragraph makes it clear that these quotations come from Shakespeare. It does not, though, make it clear which plays these quotations are from, so the parenthetical reference must include the play's titles.

The same paragraph could be somewhat reworded to make it unnecessary to include the play titles in the parenthetical references:

**In the comedy *As You Like It*, Shakespeare writes, "all the world's a stage / And all the men and women merely players" (2.7.139–40). However, this theatrical motif also plays a part in the tragedies, such as in *Macbeth*, when the tragic hero exclaims, "Life's but a walking shadow, a poor player, / That struts and frets his hour upon the stage, / And then is heard no more" (5.5.24–26).**

The first time you mention an author or title of a source in the text of the paper, use the author's full name and/or the full title of the work. After the initial reference, use only the author's last name and abbreviate longer titles:

**In *Natural Supernaturalism*, M. H. Abrams discusses the impact of the French Revolution on the Romantic writers (64). Abrams argues that these writers viewed the revolution as a "portent of universal felicity" (64).**

When referring to an entire work in general terms, it is easier to read if you identify the title and author in the text of the paper, thereby making a parenthetical reference unnecessary:

**In *Natural Supernaturalism*, M. H. Abrams discusses the various ways that Romantic poets translated mystical and religious motifs into natural phenomena in their writing.**

as opposed to:

**One critic has argued that Romantic poets translated mystical and religious motifs into natural phenomena in their writing (Abrams, *Natural Supernaturalism*).**

Remember, the MLA format is used because it makes sense. In general, use common sense when deciding how much information to include in the parenthetical references. *Strive for clarity and avoid unnecessary repetition.*

## Quoting Sources in the Text of the Paper

When quoting sources, always remember to put the passage in quotation marks and to copy it *exactly* as it appears in the original, using brackets or an ellipsis as necessary.

The MLA includes guidelines on how to quote from sources in the text of the paper:

**Quoting prose (less than 4 lines):** If you are quoting from a prose source and the quotation runs for less than four typed lines, you can include the quotation in the body of the text. There are several different ways to integrate the quotation into the text; try to alternate them to make the paper more interesting for the reader:

The quotation can come at the beginning of a sentence:

**"Whoever you are—I have always depended on the kindness of strangers," Blanche pitifully says in the final scene (*Streetcar* 178; sc. 10).**

At the end of the sentence:

**In the final scene, Blanche pitifully says, "Whoever you are—I have always depended on the kindness of strangers" (*Streetcar* 178; sc. 10).**

Or can be broken up.:

**"Whoever you are," Blanche pitifully says to the doctor, "I have always depended on the kindness of strangers" (*Streetcar* 178; sc. 10).**

When you formally introduce a quotation, meaning that it is not integrated into the sentence, precede it with a colon:

**Blanche's final words are indicative of her entire life: "I have always depended on the kindness of strangers" (*Streetcar* 178; sc. 10).**

**Quoting poetry and verse (less than 4 lines):** When you quote a single line or a part of a line of poetry or verse, place it in quotation marks in the same way you would prose.

To quote two or three lines, separate the lines with a slash (/):

**Coleridge begins his poem, "In Xanadu did Kubla Khan / A stately pleasure dome decree" (1–2).**

**Hamlet tells his mother, "So again, good night. / I must be cruel only to be kind. / Thus bad begins, and worse remains behind" (3.4.178–80).**

**Punctuation of quotations when integrated in the body of the paper:** If a sentence ends with a quotation, the punctuation at the end of the quotation (period, question mark, exclamation point) will generally remain inside the closing quotation marks:

**Blanche pleads, "I have always depended on the kindness of strangers."**

However, if a quotation ends with a period and is followed by a parenthetical reference, the period will *follow* the parenthetical reference:

**Blanche pleads, "I have always depended on the kindness of strangers" (*Streetcar* 178; sc. 10).**

If a quotation ends in a question mark or exclamation point, it will remain inside the quotation marks and a period will follow the parenthetical reference:

**Stanley howls, "Stell-lahhhh!" (*Streetcar* 66; sc. 3).**

If a quotation ends in a period and comes at the beginning or in the middle of a sentence, change the period to a comma and place it inside the quotation marks. However, exclamation points and question marks that are part of the quotation do not change and remain inside the quotation marks.

**Quoting long prose and verse passages:** Quotations of prose and verse passages of more than 4 typed lines are too long to be integrated into the text and instead are set apart. The quotation is usually first formally introduced with a sentence that ends in a colon. The quoted passage then begins on the next line, and the entire passage is indented ten spaces. When you set a passage apart, do not use any quotation marks. The parenthetical reference is placed two spaces after the quotation, following whatever punctuation ends the passage. The MLA instructs that the passage still be double-spaced.

**In the first paragraph of *The Adventures of Huckleberry Finn*, readers immediately discover Huck's distinctive voice:**

> **You don't know about me, without you have read a book by the name of "The Adventures of Tom Sawyer," but that ain't no mater. That book was made by Mr. Mark Twain, and he told the truth, mainly. (Twain 7)**

Paper Format: Documentation, Quotations, and the Bibliography/Works Cited

Follow these same general guidelines when quoting verse, but reproduce the passage as close to how it originally appears as possible, breaking up the lines in the same places as in the original. Do not use slashes to separate the lines:

**Coleridge's mariner describes the dire consequences of having killed the albatross:**
>  **Water, water, everywhere,**
>  **And all the boards did shrink;**
>  **Water, water, everywhere,**
>  **Nor any drop to drink. ("Ancient Mariner" 119–22)**

If a poem features unusual spacing of lines and words, try to reproduce it in your paper as accurately as possible:

**Much of the meaning of William Carlos Williams's "The Red Wheelbarrow" stems from how it appears on the page:**
>  **so much depends**
>  **upon**
>  **a red wheel**
>  **barrow.... (1–4)**

As with prose, you can use a three- or four-dot ellipsis when you want to omit words or phrases from within a line of poetry or verse. However, if you wish to omit an entire line or lines from a verse passage that is set off from the text, use an entire line of spaced periods to indicate the omission:

**Keats directly addresses the urn:**
>  **Thou still unravish'd bride of quietness,**
>  **Thou foster-child of silence and slow time,**
>  **. . . . . . . . . . . . . . . . . . . . . . . . . . . . . . . . . . . . . . . . . . . . . . . . . . . . . . . . . . . . . . .**
>  **What leaf-fring'd legend haunts about thy shape .....**
>  **(1–5)**

## Bibliographic and Content Notes

In addition to parenthetical references, you can also use longer supplementary notes that include additional information. In the text of the paper, you place a superscript number (raised up half a line) at the end of the sentence, which corresponds to a longer note to be found outside the text. You can either list the longer notes separately at the bottom of the page as footnotes, or group them together at the end of the paper as endnotes, whichever you prefer.

When using footnotes, leave approximately two to three inches of space at the bottom of the page. List the footnotes at the bottom of the page, beneath a solid line of about ten spaces. If the notes run long, you may continue them at the bottom of subsequent pages. Many word-processing programs make this process much easier by automatically keeping track of footnotes.

Begin endnotes on a new sheet of paper, following the conclusion of the paper and preceding the Works Cited. Group them all together, listing them in numerical order. Make certain that the numbers correspond to the superscript numbers throughout the text.

As with the parenthetical references, *all the sources listed in the supplementary notes must correspond to listings in the Works Cited.*

There are essentially two types of supplementary notes: **bibliographic** and **content.**

**Bibliographic notes** provide additional information about sources that may be too extensive to fit in the parenthetical reference. They are primarily used when several outside sources refer to one piece of information or statement in the paper and must be documented. You do not want to include more than two or three sources in a parenthetical reference because it would disrupt the flow of the writing and obstruct the reader. Instead, in the bibliographic note, which is separated from the text of the paper, you list all the outside sources, using the same format you would in a parenthetical reference but separating the various references with semicolons.

## Sample Bibliographic Notes

**A great deal of the critical material concerning *Sir Gawain and the Green Knight* has centered on the testing of Gawain at the hands of the Green Knight and Morgan le Fay.[1]**

### Endnotes
[1] **For different discussions of Gawain's testing, see Spearing, *Gawain-Poet* 191–219; Markman 170–75; Morgan 58–59; Hunt 12–15; and Green 184.**

**Content notes** provide supplementary information to or explanations of what has been discussed in the text of the paper. There might be certain material to include that, although somewhat relevant to your argument, would disrupt the flow of the text were it discussed in the body of the paper. You can use content notes to expand upon these points.

Content notes can be used for several purposes: to clarify a point of view, to provide additional background information, to evaluate various sources in more detail, or to take issue with a particular source or point of view. They are particularly useful for arguing with various critics and researchers or for helping establish your own ideas or argument as distinct from another point of view.

The MLA instructs that content notes be avoided unless absolutely necessary. Content notes are nevertheless frequently used by professionals. They are especially helpful to students, enabling them to demonstrate the extensive research they have conducted—something that instructors take into consideration when grading. This does not mean that you should use them to pad your paper with meaningless references. Don't overuse them, but do include them when they contribute something substantial to the paper.

## Sample Content Notes

Use content notes to elaborate upon or evaluate a source:

**As Bernard Spivack's work demonstrates, Iago is one of the most perplexing and fascinating figures in Shakespeare's plays.[1]**

**Notes**
**[1]In his study *Shakespeare and the Allegory of Evil*, Spivack devotes an entire book to discussing the ambiguities and mysteries of Iago's character and partly accounts for them by establishing Iago's origins in the Vice figure of morality plays.**

To provide relevant background information:

**Ibsen made a profound impression on Joyce during his youth.[1]**

**Notes**
**[1]Joyce learned Norwegian specifically to study Ibsen's plays in the original (Farrell 95), vigorously defended Ibsen against attacks by his fellow students and teachers in college (Ellmann, *James Joyce* 72–75), and wrote a review of Ibsen's play *When We Dead Awaken*, marking his beginning as a published writer (Gorman 65).**

To take issue with or counter a source or critic:

**While at Thornfield, Jane uses her imagination to escape her restlessness by transforming her experiences into a Gothic melodrama.[1]**

**Notes**
**[1]In *Jane Eyre: Portrait of a Life*, Maggie Berg argues that Jane has difficulty distinguishing fantasy from reality (55–56). But Jane does not suffer from this kind of psychotic delusion; there are**

strange goings on at Thornfield, including a madwoman locked in the attic who stabs people, sets fires, and can be heard cackling. Instead, as I argue, Jane's imagination accentuates the Gothic aspects of real events.

# The Bibliography/Works Cited List

All research papers must have a Bibliography, usually called the Works Cited list (a broader definition, referring to listings of both print and nonprint sources) that compiles all the outside sources that are introduced in the paper, giving full publication information for each. All of the parenthetical references and notes must correspond to listings in the Works Cited.

## General Guidelines

You should derive the bibliographic information from the title page or copyright page of the sources (or the cover or index of journals and periodicals). Always cite authors' names and titles *exactly* as they appear in the source. For example, if the original source uses the author's first initial rather than full name, duplicate this format in the Works Cited citation.

In general, the Works Cited list will be alphabetized according to authors' last names. If a source is written by more than one author, it will be alphabetized according to the last name of the first author listed. If there is no author, the work will be alphabetized according to the first significant word in the title. The Works Cited listing should appear on a new page following the conclusion of the paper or the endnotes.

The first line of each citation is flush with the left margin, while subsequent lines in the same citation are indented five spaces. The entire Works Cited list is double-spaced, both between lines and between citations.

## General Format for Titles

When citing titles, you should also include any subtitles; after the main title, put in a colon and then write out the complete subtitle.

Whenever you mention the title of a work—in the body of the paper, in the Works Cited listing, and even in the parenthetical references—follow the correct format and use the correct punctuation:

**Underline** titles of all major, independently published works: books, plays, long poems (book-length), newspapers, magazines, journals, movies, radio and television programs, record albums, works of art.

**Use quotation marks** for titles of all works that are published within larger works: articles, essays, short stories, short poems, short dramatic sketches, chapters of books, individual episodes of television and radio programs, songs, speeches.

Follow this punctuation even for abbreviated titles, such as in parenthetical references.

If a title of a major work appears within another title of a major work, the format is slightly more complex. Follow these general guidelines:

- Titles normally underlined within underlined titles: do not underline the primary work.
  <u>Modern Critical Interpretations</u> of Jane Eyre
- Titles normally in quotation marks within underlined titles: keep quotation marks.
  <u>Modern Critical Interpretations</u> of "Kubla Khan"
- Titles normally underlined within titles with quotation marks: keep underlined.
  "Role-Playing in Charlotte Bronte's <u>Jane Eyre</u>"
- Titles normally in quotation marks within titles with quotation marks: use single quotation marks.
  "Mysticism in Coleridge's 'Kubla Khan' "

Be careful what you capitalize in titles. In titles and subtitles, the first and last words will always be capitalized. All principal words will also be capitalized, but not definite and indefinite articles, prepositions, and conjunctions that fall in the middle of the title.

# Format for Various Citations in the Works Cited List

The MLA has set certain formats for citing sources, and the formats vary according to the type of source. The following pages provide general guidelines and list examples of the most common types of citations. However, when it comes to citing sources, there are many rules, and exceptions to rules. You should consult the MLA Handbook for more specific guidelines and for how to cite less common types of sources.

For each of the following kinds of citations, the generic pattern for the citation is laid out, followed by several sample entries. The patterns are laid out in the exact way the citation should read in a Works Cited listing, in the proper order and with the correct punctuation. Information in italics refers to specific information that will change with each source, while the bold face indicates punctuation and information that will always be included in all entries of this type.

**Book by a single author:** *Author's Last Name, First Name or Initial.* <u>Title</u>*. City of Publication: Publisher, Year of Publication.*

You can usually find the publication information on the title page or copyright page (usually on the reverse side of the title page). If there is more than one city listed, use only the first one. If the date of publication is not listed, use the latest copyright date. If several dates are listed of various printings by the same publisher, use the original publication date, but for new or revised editions, use the date of that edition. If no date of publication is listed in the book, use the abbreviation *n.d.* (no date).

The MLA Handbook lists acceptable abbreviations for various publishing houses that you can use. To cite a division or imprint of a publishing house, use a hyphen and name both (e.g., Vintage-Random House).

**Bradley, A. C.** *Shakespearean Tragedy.* **London: Macmillan, 1904.**

**Brustein, Robert.** *The Theatre of Revolt: An Approach to Modern Drama.* **Boston: Atlantic Monthly Press, 1962.**

**James, Henry.** *The Ambassadors.* **New York: New American Library, 1960.**

**Levin, Harry.** *The Question of Hamlet.* **New York: Oxford University Press, 1959.**

**O'Neill, Eugene.** *Long Day's Journey Into Night.* **New Haven: Yale University Press, 1955.**

**Supplementary information following titles:** For certain sources, you need to include additional information following the title giving more specific details:

**Editions:** If you are not using the first edition of a work, you should indicate that, identifying it in the same manner as on the title page: by number (2d ed., 3d ed., etc.), by year (1992 ed.) or as a revised edition (Rev. ed.).

**Volumes:** If you are using more than one volume from a multivolume work, indicate how many volumes are in the series (*The Norton Anthology of English Literature.* 2 vols.). However, if you are only using only one volume, only cite that volume (*The Norton Anthology of English Literature.* Vol. 2).

**Editors or Translators:** The MLA also suggests listing a book's editor or translator, if applicable. Using the abbreviations *ed.* or *trans.*, list the person's full name following the title of the book. However, if you are primarily focusing upon the translator's comments or choice of words, you should cite the work according to the translator's name, placing the abbreviation *trans.* after the translator's first name. You then put the name of the source's author after the source's title.

If a person has more than one duty, list them in the order that they appear on the title page.

Abrams, M. H., ed. *The Norton Anthology of English Literature.* 5th ed. 2 Vols. New York: Norton, 1982.

Brooks, Van Wyck. *The Ordeal of Mark Twain.* Rev. ed. New York: E. P. Dutton, 1933.

Fitzgerald, Robert, trans. *The Aeneid.* By Virgil. New York: Vintage-Random House, 1981.

Nietzsche, Friedrich. *The Birth of Tragedy and the Case of Wagner.* Trans. Walter Kaufmann. New York: Vintage-Random House, 1967.

Two or more sources by the same author:

Author's Last Name, First Name or Initial. *Title of First Book* (*in alphabetical order*). City of Publication: Publisher, Year of Publication:

———. *Title of Second Book* (*in alphabetical order*). City of Publication; Publisher, Year of Publication.

When listing more than one source by the same author, you need only list the author's name with the first citation. For each additional citation, use three hyphens and a period in place of the author's name. This indicates that the source has the same author as the one above. List the sources by the same author in alphabetical order according to the first significant word of the title. If one of the sources is an anthology or compilation edited by the same author, use the abbreviation *ed.* or *comp.* following the three hyphens.

Abrams, M. H. *Natural Supernaturalism: Tradition and Revolution in Romantic Literature.* New York: Norton, 1971.

———, ed. *The Norton Anthology of English Literature.* 5th ed. Vol. 2. New York: Norton, 1986.

Mamet, David. *Glengarry Glen Ross.* New York: Grove Press, 1982.

———. *A Life in the Theatre.* New York: Grove Press, 1977.

A book by more than one author:

*First Author's Last Name, First Name or Initial,* and *Second Author's Full Name.* <u>Title.</u> City of Publication: Publisher, Year of Publication.

When sources are written by more than one author, list the authors in the same order as they appear on the title page, separating each by a comma and writing *and* before the last name in the list. Reverse only the first author's name.

Magalaner, Marvin, and Richard M. Kain. *Joyce: The Man, the Work, the Reputation.* Westport: Greenwood Press, 1956.

If you are listing more than three authors, you need only name the first author; use the abbreviation *et al.* to indicate there are additional authors. However, if you prefer, you can list all the authors by name.

Klaus, Carl H., Miriam Gilbert, and Bradford S. Field, Jr. *Stages of Drama: Classical to Contemporary Theater.* Glenview: Scott, Foresman and Company, 1981.

or:

Klaus, Carl H., et al. *Stages of Drama: Classical to Contemporary Theater.* Glenview: Scott, Foresman and Company, 1981.

### Anthologies/Compilations:

*Editor's Last Name, First Name or Initial,* **ed. [or comp.]** *Title.* City of Publication: Publisher, Year of Publication.

If you are citing an entire anthology or compilation (and not just a single work from it), list the citation according to the last name of the editor or compiler, using the abbreviation *ed.* or *comp.* following the name.

Bloom, Harold, ed. *Modern Critical Interpretations: Charlotte Bronte's* Jane Eyre. New York: Chelsea House, 1987.

Graham, Don, ed. *Critical Essays on Frank Norris.* Boston: G. K. Hall, 1980.

Marranca, Bonnie, ed. *American Dreams: The Imagination of Sam Shepard.* New York: Performing Arts Journal Publications, 1981.

### A work within an anthology or collection:

*Author's Last Name, Author's First Name or Initial.* "Title of Work Within Anthology." *[Title is normally in quotation marks unless originally published as a book.] Title of Anthology.* **Ed.** Editor's Full Name. City of Publication: Publisher, Year of Publication. Inclusive pages of work within the Anthology.

Eagleton, Terry. "*Jane Eyre*: A Marxist Study." *Modern Critical Interpretations: Charlotte Bronte's* Jane Eyre. Ed. Harold Bloom. New York: Chelsea House, 1987. 29–45.

Melville, Herman. *Billy Budd. Selected Tales and Poems by Herman Melville.* Ed. Richard Chase. New York: Holt Rinehart, 1950. 289–376.

Mendelson, Edward. "The Sacred, The Profane and *The Crying of Lot 49.*" *Individual and Community: Variations on a Theme in American Fiction.* Ed. Kenneth H. Baldwin and David K. Kirby. Durham: Duke University Press, 1978. 182–222.

If you are citing several works from one anthology or collection, you do not have to repeat the full publication information for each. Include a full citation for the entire collection and use cross-references for the individual works you wish to cite within it. For the cross-references, list the editor's last name of the collection and the relevant page numbers following the title of the individual work:

**Bloom, Harold, ed.** *Modern Critical Interpretations: Charlotte Bronte's* Jane Eyre. **New York: Chelsea House, 1987.**
**Eagleton, Terry. "***Jane Eyre:* **A Marxist Study." Bloom 29–45.**

### An introduction, preface, foreword, or afterword:

*Last Name of Author [of introduction, preface, etc.], First Name or Initial. Name of part of book being cited [e.g., Introduction].* <u>Title of Complete Work.</u> *By Author of Complete Work. City of Publication: Publisher, Year of Publication. Inclusive pages of part within the complete work.*

Cite an introduction, preface, foreword or afterword according to the author of that specific part. Then identify the part of the work by name (introduction, preface, etc.), followed by the title and author or editor of the complete work.

**Kermode, Frank. Introduction.** *The Tragedy of Hamlet, Prince of Denmark.* **By William Shakespeare.** *The Riverside Shakespeare.* **Ed. G. Blakemore Evans. Boston: Houghton Mifflin, 1974. 1135–40.**

**Sale, William M., Jr. Introduction.** *Pamela or Virtue Rewarded.* **By Samuel Richardson. New York: Norton, 1958. v–xiv.**

**Wetzsteon, Ross. Introduction. Fool for Love** *and Other Plays.* **By Sam Shepard. New York: Bantam, 1984. 1–15.**

### An anonymous title:

<u>Title.</u> *City of Publication: Publisher, Year of Publication.*

If the author of a source is anonymous or unknown, cite the book beginning with the title, and alphabetize it within the Works Cited by the first significant word in the title.

***The Owl and the Nightingale.*** **Trans. Brian Stone. New York: Penguin, 1971.**

### An article in a newspaper:

*Last Name of Author of Article, First Name or Initial. "Title of Article."* <u>Name of Newspaper</u> *Date Month Year, edition [if applicable]: page/section numbers.*

If it is not clear which city a newspaper comes from, put the city and state in brackets following the name of the newspaper. This is not necessary, however, for national newspapers, such as *USA Today*. If applicable, include the specific edition (morning, evening, late, etc.). Use abbreviations for months. Try to give as specific page numbers as possible, including section numbers or letters as well as pages.

**Gussow, Mel. "The Daring Visions of Four New Young Playwrights."** *New York Times* **13 Feb. 1977, sec. 2:1–13.**

**Schmitt, Eric. "Army Women Face Bias on Macho Base."** *New York Times* **2 Aug. 1992, late ed.: 28 L.**

### An article in a magazine:
*Last Name of Author of Article, First Name or Initial. "Title of Article." Name of Magazine Date and/or Month Year: pages.*

For weekly or biweekly magazines, include the complete date. For monthly magazines, just include the month (or months) and the year.

**Turque, Bill, et al. "The War for the West: Fighting for the Soul of America's Mythic Land." *Newsweek* 30 Sept. 1991:18–35.**

**VerMeulen, Michael. "Sam Shepard: Yes, Yes, Yes." *Esquire* Feb. 1980:79–81, 85–86.**

### An article in a journal:
*Last Name of Author of Article, First Name or Initial. "Title of Article." Name of Journal Volume and/or Issue Number (Year): page numbers.*

Most scholarly journals are grouped together in bound volumes. For these journals, each issue will have a volume number and an issue number (within the larger volume). If a journal numbers its pages continuously throughout the entire volume, you do not need to include this issue number; the volume number will be sufficient to indicate the source's location. However, if each issue is paginated separately (meaning that each begins with page one), then you need to list both the volume and issue number (separated by a period). Get the volume number from the cover of the journal of the bound volume's spine.

As long as the journal does have a volume number, you never need to give a more specific date than the year. You can ignore days and months, even if they are listed on the cover of the journal.

Again, let common sense be your guide; include the information necessary for the reader to locate the source without a problem.

**Ceynowa, Andrzej. "The Dramatic Structure of *Dutchman*." *Black American Literature Forum* 17.1 (1983):15–18.**

**Hall, Jean. "The Socialized Imagination: Shelley's *The Cenci* and *Prometheus Unbound*." *Studies in Romanticism* 23 (1984):339–50**

**Mackenzie, Manfred. "Ironic Melodrama in *The Portrait of a Lady*," *Modern Fiction Studies* 12 (1966):7–23.**

**Putzel, Steven. "Expectation, Confutation, Revelation: Audience Complicity in the Plays of Sam Shepard." *Modern Drama* 30 (1987):147–60.**

**Storey, Robert. "The Making of David Mamet." *Hollins Critic* 16.4 (1979):1–11.**

# Typing the Paper

You've worked hard on your paper, and it deserves to be read. So make certain your reader can read it. Always type the paper and try to do it as neatly as possible. Don't hand in a paper covered with White-Out, erasure marks, and pencil scrawling. Neatness always counts and makes a big impression; your instructor will recognize the care you've put into your paper and treat it with more respect.

Term papers should be double-spaced throughout. Always use white paper measuring 8½ × 11 inches. Leave a one-inch margin on the top and bottom of the pages, as well as on the right and left sides. Begin each paragraph by indenting five spaces.

Make certain you number the pages consecutively throughout the paper. Place page numbers one-half inch down from the top, in the upper right-hand corner. Put your last name before each page number in case the pages somehow become separated.

*And always keep a copy of your paper!*

# The Title Page

The MLA does not recommend that you include a title page on your paper but instead suggest that you include all of the relevant information on the first page of your paper. To follow the MLA format, skip one inch on the first page and, flush left, type your name, your instructor's name, the course, and the date on separate lines. Then skip two lines and center the title of the paper. Do not underline the title or put it in quotation marks.

If your instructor does not insist otherwise, you may want to include a title page. Many instructors find them helpful because they make it easier to identify the writer and also provide space for comments.

If you choose to include a title page, use a blank sheet of paper and center the title of the paper about one third down from the top. Then skip down another third and include your name, your instructor's name, the course, and the date centered on separate lines. Do not put a page number on the cover; begin numbering the pages on the first page of the paper, inside the cover, which will be page one.

When choosing the title for your paper, you can be as creative as you like as long as you make the paper's topic extremely clear. Most titles begin with a short phrase or a quotation followed by a colon and a longer sentence that explains the paper's topic in greater detail.

## Examples of Titles

"Mad North-North West": Madness and the Social Order in Shakespeare's Tragedies

"I Have a Dream": The Vision of Martin Luther King Jr. as It Exists Today

On the Brink of Disaster: The Economic Implications of the Destruction of the Rain Forest

# IX.

# Write Stuff: The Mechanics of Good Writing

All of the information and guidelines included so far have been preparing you for this moment. It's time to begin writing.

As was emphasized in the first chapter, the most important part of any paper is the quality of the ideas conveyed in it. All the preparation and work you have been doing up until now should have helped you to come up with brilliant, innovative, and powerful ideas for your paper. Now, as you begin to write, your primary goal is to convey those ideas effectively.

This chapter includes some general guidelines on the mechanics of writing that will help you to better communicate your ideas on paper. However, one of the best ways to improve your writing is by reading. As you conduct research for various papers and are exposed to more and more scholarly writing, you'll develop a better understanding of and appreciation for what makes good writing. Moreover, you'll begin to integrate certain stylistic traits into your own work.

# The Writing Process

As this book has probably made clear to you, preparing a term paper is a process that proceeds in stages. The same principle holds true for the actual writing of the paper.

Many people have difficulty writing because they have been taught to write in a manner that emphasizes only the final product, which is supposed to be flawless. When students first begin writing, this concern about creating a perfect final product creates enormous pressure; unable to achieve perfection on the first try, these students virtually freeze up. They lose sight of their own ideas, which get buried beneath mounds of grammatical rules and terms.

Good writing takes time and effort to produce. Even after having conducted research and prepared an outline, you can't expect to zip off the perfect paper on the first try. Many factors go into producing quality writing, and it's impossible to keep track of them all at the same time. That's why successful writers have learned to write in stages, reworking the paper in several drafts before proclaiming it a final product.

You should follow their lead and rewrite your paper several times, each time concentrating upon a different aspect:

**1. First Draft:** One of the most difficult parts of writing is beginning. Trying to include all the information you need to is not an easy task. If you also concern yourself with making it flawless right from the start, you're building an extra hurdle for yourself, making it all the more difficult to take that one giant leap into the physical process of writing.

While correct grammar and spelling are important because they make the paper more readable, they do not have to be your primary concerns at this point. Grammar can be corrected anytime, but without a solid foundation of strong ideas, all the perfectly phrased sentences in the world aren't going to make a good paper.

In the first draft, you only need to concentrate on getting your ideas out and integrating your notes from secondary sources. This eliminates any stress about the actual process of writing, particularly any preoccupation or anxiety over grammatical rules, and leaves you free to concentrate on conveying your ideas. Remember, this is for your eyes only; don't worry yet about how it sounds or looks.

Following your outline and referring to your note cards, start at the beginning of the paper and simply start writing. Keep on writing until you reach the end of the paper, without stopping or going back to make changes. Don't worry about grammar or spelling yet. If you find you hit a roadblock—a point in the paper where you freeze and do not know what to write—just mark the point with an X and move on. You can go back later and work on the trouble spot.

This will be an extremely rough draft—choppy and somewhat difficult to read. That's okay, though. It's only a draft. By getting all the ideas and information out and in one place, however, you are giving yourself raw material you can then work with and refine. That's something you can't do with a blank sheet of paper.

**2. Subsequent Drafts:** Once you have completed your first draft, go back to the beginning of the paper and rewrite it. You should continue to rewrite the paper as many times as necessary. The paper will improve with each rewrite.

In the first few drafts, you should concentrate upon *revising*, and in the latter ones, upon *refining* and *editing*.

When you revise the paper, you address the paper as a whole and focus on the *content*—the ideas and major points that are expressed within the paper. Make certain all your ideas are clearly and fully explained, that nothing is left ambiguous or only partly stated and that there are no gaps in the argument. Also, examine the overall organization of the paper, making certain that one point flows smoothly and logically into the next. If necessary, move portions of the paper around to see where they fit within the overall structure. Check that everything in the paper supports the thesis statement, and take out anything that detracts from the argument.

Between revisions, read over what you have written and take notes so that you can make changes in future revisions. You want to read from an objective standpoint, as if you are a first-time reader of your paper. Try to distance yourself from your writing so that you can evaluate it from a critical perspective. Ask yourself probing questions: Is everything explained fully? Will the reader be able to understand everything as it is laid out here? Are there any holes or gaps in the argument, such as ideas that are not fully developed or only partially explained? Does one idea flow smoothly into the next, with no disruptions in logic? Try to anticipate the questions a reader might have upon reading the paper as it stands, and then include the answers in your next revision. This will ensure that you prove your thesis.

Because you are so closely tied to your paper it might be difficult to be an objective reader of it. Think of yourself as a newspaper editor, going over an article by one of your reporters. As an editor, it's your job to make certain that everyone reading the newspaper will be able to understand the article and that every point in it is explained. Also, try reading it out loud and listening to how it sounds when spoken.

It's always a good idea to leave the paper aside for a day or two once you think it's complete. After you've been away from it, you'll be able to approach it from a fresher perspective. Very often, you'll see problems in the paper you were not previously aware of, or come up with innovative ways to restructure or rewrite passages that trouble you.

After you are comfortable with the content of the paper—that is, you believe that all your ideas are explained fully and clearly and that the overall structure of the paper is solid—you can begin refining it. Refining the paper involves concentrating upon the writing itself and paying attention to how things are phrased. Read through the paper focusing on individual sentence and paragraph structure. Think about ways you might rephrase various sentences to make them more powerful and interesting, without being overly flashy or wordy.

**3. Final Draft:** When you are satisfied with the content and writing of the paper, you are ready to edit it. When you edit the paper, you proofread it for grammar, punctuation, and spelling errors. You only need to edit in the final draft. Of course, throughout the entire process of rewriting a paper, you can always correct any errors you spot, but it isn't necessary to make reading for correctness your primary concern until the final draft.

When editing the final draft, read the paper through very slowly and carefully, examining it word by word, sentence by sentence, and paragraph by paragraph. You may want to read through it several times, one time looking for spelling errors, another time for grammatical errors, etc. Have resources, such as a dictionary or grammar handbook, close at hand, and double check *anything* that you are not one hundred percent certain is correct.

It's very easy to use the wrong word for something. We often have a sense of what a particular word means, but, confusing it with another word, we accidentally use it in an incorrect manner. To avoid making this mistake, double-check definitions of any complex words you might have included. Make certain that you used your words in the correct manner.

When going over the final draft, you should also double-check your formatting. Make certain you have cited all your sources and that you have used the proper format.

Since you have an extremely close connection to your paper, finding errors may be difficult. You have looked at the same pages so many times that many errors may escape your attention. *Read very carefully, concentrating on each word.* If at all possible, try to get someone else to read over your paper as well. He or she might be able to pick up on errors you have overlooked.

When you have completed editing and have corrected all errors, type up or print out the final version of the paper. You should always proofread the final version, the paper that you intend to hand in, to ensure that the final copy is neat, complete, and in the proper order. And *always* keep a copy of it. More than one teacher has been known to misplace a paper.

# Sentences and Paragraphs:
# Solid Structure and Smooth Flow

## Sentence Patterns

There are various types of sentences, ranging from the simple to the complex, the declarative to the exclamatory. To make the paper more interesting to read, it is extremely important that you vary the kind of sentence you use. If you do not, the paper will be monotonous and choppy, as in the following:

> **The ghost tells Hamlet that Claudius murdered him. Hamlet stages a play in order to "catch the conscience of the King" (II.ii.605). Claudius jumps up in the middle of the play. Hamlet believes Claudius is guilty. Hamlet tries to plot his revenge.**

In the above passage, all the sentences follow a similar pattern, beginning with the subject of the sentence, which makes the writing sound flat and repetitive.

Although the various sentence patterns are defined by grammatical terms, you do not necessarily have to know the terminology. From your reading of scholarly material, you'll develop an "ear" for various sentence patterns and begin to use them in your own writing. If you do wish to learn more about sentence types, consult a grammar or writing handbook.

There are several easy ways you can vary sentence types without having to study sentence patterns in detail:
• Alternate the lengths of various sentences, making some short and crisp, others more complex and sophisticated:

> **After the ghost reveals that Claudius murdered him, Hamlet stages a play in order to "catch the conscience of the King" (II.ii.605). In the midst of the play, Claudius jumps up and races from the room, confirming his guilt in Hamlet's eyes. Hamlet now plots his revenge.**

However, be careful to avoid fragments and run-ons (see below).
• Join shorter sentences together using either a conjunction (*and, but, or,* etc.):

> **The ghost tells Hamlet that Claudius murdered him, but Hamlet is still plagued by doubts.**

or a semicolon:

> **Hamlet's greatest adversary is his own conscience; plagued by doubts, he cannot take action.**

Only use a semicolon if the two sentences are very closely related, and make certain that the relationship between the two is clear to the reader.
• Alternate where you begin various sentences. For example, you do not want to begin every sentence with the subject because it sounds too choppy and repetitive. You can instead start sentences with phrases or clauses that modify or describe the subject:

> **Believing that Claudius killed his father, Hamlet stages a play to "catch the conscience of the King" (II.ii.605).**

> **After watching the play that Hamlet has so carefully staged, Claudius jumps out of his seat and runs from the room.**

• One particularly easy way to ensure you have a variety of sentence patterns is to change the way you introduce various quotations. As we saw before, you can place quotations at the beginning or end of the sentence, or split them up (see chapter on Paper Format).

## The Well-Structured Paragraph

In many ways, a well-structured paragraph is merely a smaller version of the paper as a whole. Like your entire paper, each paragraph should focus upon a single idea, and everything in the paragraph should support it.

In a standard paragraph, a *topic sentence,* usually the first sentence, will summarize the main idea of the paragraph. Just as all the points in the body of the paper must support the thesis statement, all the sentences in a paragraph must relate to the topic sentence. Any sentences that do not relate to the topic sentence will distract the reader and detract from your argument; they should be moved or deleted. Although not always necessary, it is also a good idea to include a concluding sentence at the end of the paragraph that summarizes what has preceded and leads into the next paragraph.

The following is an example of a well-developed, standard paragraph (italics added):

*The Duke in* Measure for Measure *seems to be modeled upon Hamlet, because they both employ theatrical devices as a means of taking action.* Just as Hamlet decides to "put an antic disposition on" (I.v.172), enabling him to scrutinize and test those around him, the Duke adopts the habit of a friar in order to observe Angelo, as he says, to "behold his sway" (I.iii.43). Similarly, Hamlet stages a play to "catch the conscience of the King" (II.ii.605), while the Duke, echoing Hamlet's claim to be only "mad in craft" (III.iv.189), says he must match "craft against vice" (III.ii.281) and conceives of an elaborate scene, complete with costumed characters playing roles, in which he ensnares Angelo. *Both Hamlet and the Duke thereby view theatricality as a kind of weapon at their disposal by which they may use and test those around them.*

— *Topic Sentence*

↑

*Examples To Support Topic Sentence*

↓

*Summary Sentence*

This standard format is an extremely effective means of constructing a paragraph; it ensures that your writing remains focused on specific points. It also forces you to lay out explicitly your ideas for the reader. Not all paragraphs must follow this standard format, however. For example, you do not necessarily have to include a topic sentence, particularly if it is clear how a paragraph follows from the one preceding it or if the main idea uniting all the points of the paragraph is blatant and self-evident.

*Always make certain that all the points within the paragraph relate to the same main idea and that one paragraph flows smoothly into the next.*

# Smooth Flow:
## Between Sentences and Paragraphs

As the writer of your paper, it's your job to act as tour guide for the reader. As you ease the reader through the complexities of your argument, journeying from one main point to the next, you want to follow as smooth a path as possible, so that by the paper's end the reader will have enjoyed the trip and not feel disoriented.

You must therefore work to create as straight and clear a path as possible. This means that each sentence and paragraph, from first to last, must flow smoothly and logically into the next.

You will probably be able to establish a relatively straightforward argument simply by placing the sentences and paragraphs in logical order and by deleting anything that does not support the thesis or topic sentences. However, you will also have to reword or rephrase certain sentences in order to establish the connections between various ideas.

This can often be done by adding a key word or phrase that implies the relationship between the sentences. For example, the following two sentences do not appear to follow one another because the connection between the two is not explicit:

**Ending with the violent deaths of its two young lovers, *Romeo and Juliet* is usually considered a tragedy. It contains a number of humorous and absurd elements that are typical of a Shakespearean comedy.**

By simply adding a key transitional word (here shown in italics), the relationship between the two becomes clear:

**Ending with the violent deaths of its two young lovers, *Romeo and Juliet* is usually considered a tragedy. However, it also contains a number of humorous and absurd elements that are typical of a Shakespearean comedy.**

There are many transitional words and phrases you can use to interconnect various sentences, including the following:

**To build upon previous sentence:** *and, also, additionally, as a result, consequently, further, furthermore, in addition, moreover*
**To compare with previous sentence:** *similarly, in the same manner, likewise, at the same time, by the same token*
**To contrast with previous sentence:** *however, but, in contrast, nevertheless, although, yet, on the other hand*
**To summarize or draw a conclusion:** *therefore, in other words, in short, to sum up, thus*

It is particularly important that paragraphs flow smoothly from one to the next. You need to phrase each topic sentence so that it not only summarizes the main idea of that particular paragraph but also indicates its relationship to the preceding one. If necessary, you can precede a topic sentence with a transitional sentence that bridges the two paragraphs:

*Summary Sentence (Previous Paragraph)*
*Bridge To Link Paragraphs*
*Topic Sentence*

... Hamlet and the Duke thereby both demonstrate a flair for the theatrical.

*Despite their similar employment of theatrical devices, Hamlet and the Duke differ significantly in their beliefs.* The Duke demonstrates an understanding of the inherent theatricality of human experience that Hamlet seems to lack.

# Watch Out:
## Common Errors in Grammar and Language Usage

As we have been emphasizing, ideas are the most important part of your paper. However, correct grammar is considered an important feature of academic writing; it makes the paper more readable and indicates a professional attitude on the part of the writer.

There are an infinite amount of grammatical rules, and no one can learn them all. Just as we learn to speak without learning the "rules" of conversation but by listening to those around us, we can also learn about grammar and proper language usage by reading. The more you read, the more you will develop an "ear" for correct grammar. Then when you write, mistakes in grammar will just not sound right. Learn to trust your ear and to phrase things so they "sound" correct. If, however, you have a serious problem with grammar, you may need to make an extra effort to improve. Many grammar workbooks are available that can help. You might also want to talk with your instructor about additional tutoring.

The following is a brief list of some of the errors in grammar, punctuation, and language usage that frequently appear in student papers:

**1. Sentence fragments:** A sentence fragment is a group of words that does not function as a complete sentence. A complete sentence must consist of a full independent clause—a group of words that includes a subject and verb and can stand on its own.

The most common types of sentence fragments are those that do not contain subjects or verbs. Others are less easy to spot, such as subordinate clauses and phrases that cannot stand alone and need to be a part of a sentence in order to make sense.

**Examples of sentence fragments:**
**We drove to the store. And got gas.**
                    **No Subject**

**Everyone did well in school. Not Ellen.**
                    **No Verb**

**We will be very lucky. If we win the lottery.**
                  **Subordinate Clause**

**Although it might rain. The beach will be nice.**
**Subordinate Clause**

**Susan did the crossword puzzle. Eating her bacon and eggs.**
          **Verbal Phrase (Modifies Susan)**

**They loved taking vacations. But hated coming home.**
          **Part of a Compound Predicate**

Sentence fragments can usually be joined to surrounding sentences, often by making simple changes such as by adding a comma. However, you may sometimes need to rework the fragment to make it a complete sentence:

**We drove to the store and got gas.**
**Everyone did well in school, except for Ellen.**
**Eating her bacon and eggs, Susan did the crossword puzzle.**
**They loved taking vacations but hated coming home.**

**2. Run-on sentences:** Run-ons are the opposite of fragments. While a fragment does not contain an independent clause, a run-on contains too many. Run-on sentences string along one clause or phrase after the other, serving to confuse the reader:

***Hamlet* is about a young prince who wants to take revenge for his father's murder but he is plagued by doubts so he can't take any action so he decides to stage a play to confirm the guilt of the alleged murderer.**

As this example demonstrates, the reader can easily get lost in the muddle of a run-on, losing its logical thread. The above sentence could easily be divided into two or three shorter sentences, making it much easier to read:

***Hamlet* is about a young prince who wants to take revenge for his father's murder. Plagued by doubts, he cannot take action. He therefore decides to stage a play to confirm the guilt of the alleged murderer.**

**3. Pronoun-antecedent agreement:** Pronouns (*he, she, him, her, his, hers, their, theirs, it, its*) take the place of nouns, and the nouns to which they refer are called antecedents. Pronouns and antecedents must always agree, meaning they must both either be singular or plural:

**Jeff wrote his paper. (Singular)**
**The students wrote their papers. (Plural)**

There are two cases that are extremely problematic: indefinite pronouns and generic nouns. An indefinite pronoun refers to a nonspecific person or thing (*anybody, anyone, each, either, everybody, everything, neither, none, someone,* etc.), while a generic noun represents a typical member of a group (*a lawyer, a student, an American,* etc.). Although it may not always seem so, both of these antecedents are always followed by singular pronouns. You should either use "he or she" as the pronoun, or rewrite the sentence to avoid the problem.

**Incorrect:**
**When everyone has finished their essay, the class is dismissed.**
**Correct:**
**When everyone has finished his or her essay, the class is dismissed.**
**Or**
**When the students have finished their essays, the class is dismissed.**

**Incorrect:**
**A teacher must be considerate of their students' needs.**
**Correct:**
**A teacher must be considerate of his or her students' needs.**
**Or**
**Teachers must be considerate of their students' needs.**

**4. Dangling Modifiers:** Modifiers are single words or phrases that describe or elaborate upon some other word. Dangling modifiers do not logically refer to any word in the sentence and make it incoherent. Be particularly careful if a sentence begins with a modifier, because whatever subject follows *must* be the one to which the modifier refers:

**Published after O'Neill's death, many critics consider *Long Day's Journey Into Night* his best play.**

In the above sentence, the modifier "Published after his death" refers to *Long Day's Journey Into Night,* not to the "many critics." It should be phrased:

**Published after O'Neill's death, *Long Day's Journey Into Night* is considered his best play by many critics.**

**5. Split infinitives:** An infinitive form of a verb consists of two parts—the word *to* plus the verb (*to eat, to sleep,* etc.). An infinitive is "split" when another word comes between the two parts.

Although certain constructions featuring split infinitives have come to be accepted in the language, split infinitives usually sound awkward and disrupt the flow of the sentence. In general, try to avoid splitting infinitives.

**Split Infinitive:**
**Rochester tries to continually propose to Jane.**

**Not Split / Better Rephrased:**
**Rochester continually tries to propose to Jane.**

**6. Homophones:** Homophones are words that sound alike but have different spellings and meanings. As they sound similar, they are extremely easy to confuse in your writing. Even when you carefully proofread, homophones can often escape your detection.

Some of the most commonly confused homophones are:

| your/you're | its/it's | there/their |
| whose/who's | two/too | |

When you proofread, look out for any homophones and make certain that you have the correct word on paper.

**7. Affect/Effect:** Many writers tend to confuse the words *affect* and *effect*. In general, *affect* is used as a verb, meaning "to influence" or "to change":

**The heat *affects* my ability to work.**

And *effect* is used as a noun, meaning "result":

**The heat has a disruptive *effect* on my work.**

However, *effect* can also be used as a verb when it means "to make possible," "to cause," or "to accomplish":

**Heat *effects* certain changes in my work habits.**

**8. Ambiguous references:** Broad references, such as *this*, *that*, *which*, and *it*, are ambiguous and can be confusing to the reader. You should clearly indicate the person, subject, or idea to which these refer.

**Ambiguously Phrased:**
**Rochester tells Jane he is already married. This changes our perspective of him.**

**More Clearly Phrased As:**
**Rochester tells Jane he is already married. This *revelation* changes our perspective of him.**

**9. Sentences ending in prepositions:** Prepositions are certain words, usually appearing at the beginning of a phrase, that are used to describe or to elaborate on some other word in the sentence.

There are a limited number of prepositions in the English language. You should become familiar with them; some of the most common include: *about, above, across, after, against, along, among, around, as, at, before, behind, below, beside, between, but, by, concerning, considering, despite, down, during, except, for, from, in, inside, into, like, near, next, of, off, on, onto, out, over, past, plus, regarding, respecting, since, than, through, throughout, to, toward, under, underneath, unlike, until, unto, up, upon, with, without.*

It is considered grammatically incorrect to end a sentence with a preposition. If a sentence ends in a preposition, rephrase it.

**Incorrect:**
   **The student did not know what the teacher's question referred to.**

**Correct:**
   **The student did not know to what the teacher's question referred.**

## Language and Style

Just as important a consideration as the structure of sentences and paragraphs is your use of language. Words are powerful entities. Not only do they convey specific meanings, but they also carry additional implications and associations that can achieve varying effects. Choose your words carefully.

What follows are several points involving style and language that you should keep in your mind as you write your paper.

## Evenness of Tone

Tone refers to the style or manner in which something is written. It reflects a particular attitude toward the material and signals to readers how they are meant to respond. The tone of a work can vary from being extremely serious to sarcastic, to silly or humorous.

A good writer will match the tone of a piece to his or her intended audience. For example, an article about the 1992 presidential campaign that appears in a rock music magazine like *Rolling Stone* will certainly have a different tone than one appearing in a serious news weekly such as *Time*.

Obviously, your research paper will be written in a different tone than the more casual one you might use in everyday conversation or in a letter to a friend. While in those venues, colloquialisms (casual expressions used in everyday conversation) are acceptable; in a research paper they detract from the seriousness of the venue. You should avoid using colloquialisms, especially clichés (trite expressions that have been used so frequently they have become commonplace and mundane) and slang (words or expressions that are not considered standard English and have fallen into popular usage).

At the same time, don't go to the other extreme. Very often, students, in attempting to sound more intellectual and to impress the instructor, will overshoot the mark and *overwrite,* filling the paper with long, complicated words and antiquated expressions. Rather than sounding sophisticated or scholarly, this only makes the paper too wordy and the writer seem pompous and insincere.

**Too Conversational:**

**In *Hamlet*, Shakespeare's coolest play, things start to really happen after the ghost lets the cat out of the bag. The ghost tells Hamlet that he was offed by Hamlet's uncle. And boy, does that freak Hamlet out.**

**Too Wordy and Highbrow:**

**In *Hamlet*, the play many consider to be Shakespeare's most titillating and resplendent dramatic work, events are perpetuated by a singular happening of sublime and epic proportions. The phantom, that translucent visitor from the world beyond, makes a startling revelation: he has met his unnatural demise through the machinations of his own flesh and blood.**

Of course, these two passages are extreme examples of tonal differences and are meant to demonstrate the inappropriateness of these styles in a research paper. However, you can occasionally utilize a particular tone for effect. For example, if you want to point out the absurdity of some event in a play, you might describe it in colloquial terms. This should only be done for effect and only on occasion.

The most serious error you can make is to create an uneven tone that confuses the reader:

**Things start to happen in *Hamlet* after a happening of sublime and epic proportions, when the ghost makes the startling reve-**

**lation that he's been offed by Hamlet's uncle. The news thus freaks Hamlet out.**

The above passage includes slang terms and colloquialisms intermixed with more complex, scholarly language. When the tone is uneven like this, the reader does not know how to interpret the passage. Is the author poking fun at *Hamlet* or trying to discuss it seriously?

Even individual words and expressions can disrupt the overall tone:

**The ghost reveals the circumstances of his death thusly.**

**The action of the play is thereby set in motion by the ghost's freaky revelation.**

In the above lines, "thusly," a scholarly term, and "freaky," a colloquialism, disrupt the tone of the sentence and jar the reader.

Instead of writing at extremes or intermixing styles, you want to maintain an even tone throughout the paper.

**Proper, Even Tone:**
**A supernatural event sets the action of *Hamlet* in motion. The ghost reveals to Hamlet the circumstances surrounding his death, claiming that he has been murdered by his brother, Hamlet's uncle. This startling revelation shocks and dismays the young Hamlet.**

In general, if you have conceived the kinds of powerful and innovative ideas you should have, they will stand perfectly well on their own, without needing the help of flashy or highbrow language. Try to explain your ideas in a simple and straightforward manner but without being too casual or conversational.

## Varying Word Choice—Using a Thesaurus

To make your paper interesting to read, you should try to vary your choice of words as much as possible. Be extremely careful that you do not use the same word or similar forms of a word too frequently, because this makes the paper repetitive and tedious.

To help increase the variety of your word choices, you should use a *thesaurus*, a special type of dictionary that compiles synonyms (words that have the same meaning as a particular word). Try to find a thesaurus that is organized like a dictionary, with words listed in alphabetical order and their possible synonyms beneath them.

When you edit the paper, look for repetitions of the same words, especially those that appear close together, such as in the same paragraph. You can then look up the word in the thesaurus and choose an alternative.

For example, the following passage unnecessarily repeats the same words and phrases:

> **Shakespeare's comedies feature many humorous moments. Filled with many humorous moments, *The Comedy of Errors* is particularly humorous. The confusion between the sets of twins results in a great deal of humorous fun.**

The passage can easily be changed and made more interesting by using synonyms:

> **Shakespeare's comedies feature many humorous moments. Filled with comical scenes, *The Comedy of Errors* is particularly amusing. The confusion between the sets of twins results in a great deal of hilarity.**

When using a thesaurus, be careful which synonym you choose. A synonym might have a slightly different definition than the original word or carry a different connotation (a suggested or implied meaning other than the official definition). If necessary, look up the definition in the dictionary to make certain it works in your sentence.

Many synonyms listed in the thesaurus are outmoded and not frequently used in writing. If you include them in your paper, they will appear strange and disrupt the evenness of tone. You should therefore choose only those synonyms with which you are already familiar and are comfortable using in your writing.

Of course, certain words are limited in the number of their synonyms, and you might have to repeat the same word several times. If at all possible, cut down your usage of that word and include it only when absolutely necessary.

## Staying Active—Avoiding the Passive Voice

Passive constructions remove the action of the sentence from the present moment or from the subject of the sentence. They consist of a form of the verb *to be* joined with some other verb:

**The hill was climbed by Jack and Jill.**
**Poor grades are received by poor students.**

Overuse of the passive voice can make writing wordy and mundane. One of the easiest ways to improve writing is to change passive constructions into active ones.

To do this, rewrite the sentence so that the subject of the sentence initiates the action, rather than receives it:

**Jack and Jill <u>climbed</u> the hill.**
**Poor students <u>receive</u> poor grades.**

To make a sentence active, you may have to rework it extensively. For example, you might have to introduce a subject that has been merely implied:

Passive:

**A ghost <u>was seen</u> during the watch.**

**The theatrical motif <u>is</u> firmly established in the opening lines of the play.**

Active:

**The guards <u>saw</u> a ghost during their watch.**

**Shakespeare firmly <u>establishes</u> the theatrical motif in the opening lines of the play.**

Be particularly careful to avoid the phrases "it is" and "it was," especially when they appear at the beginning of the sentence. These ambiguous constructions can almost always be replaced by more active, more specific terms.

Passive:

**<u>It is</u> discovered that a ghost had appeared to the sentinels.**
**<u>It was</u> revealed that the sword was poisoned.**

Active:

**Hamlet <u>discovers</u> that a ghost had appeared to the sentinels.**
**Laertes <u>reveals</u> that his sword was poisoned.**

## Using Nondiscriminatory Language

In recent years, the problem of discriminatory language has become an important issue in writing. For ethical reasons, your writing must not stereotype or demean any individuals or groups. This refers not only to the content of your writing but to the style of language and the words you use.

Using nondiscriminatory language extends beyond avoiding derogatory and insulting terms to describe various people. In general, you need to avoid making any kind of assumption or generalization about people, especially concerning ethnicity and race, gender and sexual orientation, political and religious belief, and economic or class associations.

Unless it is necessary for your argument, you should not identify or categorize people according to their gender, origins, personal beliefs, and affiliations because this is considered discriminatory. For example, if you are writing a paper about Asian-Americans, you might then identify Amy Tan as a successful Chinese-American author. However, if you are writing a paper about contemporary novelists, Amy Tan's ethnicity and origins are irrelevant and bringing it up can be construed as discriminatory.

One of the most prominent forms of discrimination in writing is the use of sexist language. Again, sexism goes beyond using derogatory terms to describe men and women. Anytime you needlessly identify a person by gender, you are discriminating by sex. Unless a person's gender is relevant to your paper, you do not need to discuss it. It is not necessary to say that "Shakespeare was a man who knew how to write brilliantly"; you need only say, "Shakespeare was a brilliant writer."

Words containing "man" and "men" are often used in a generic fashion to refer to both men and women. These words should be changed to be non-gender specific, making them neutral and applicable to both sexes.

Here are some examples:

| Discriminatory: | Change to: |
| --- | --- |
| chairman | chairperson |
| policeman | police officer |
| workman | worker, laborer |
| mankind | people, humans |
| to man | to operate |

Similarly, masculine pronouns (*he, him, his*) are often used to indicate unnamed persons of either sex. In order to rephrase these sentences in nonsexist terms, you can either change all masculine pronouns to include both sexes (*he or she, him or her*), or rewrite the sentence using plural pronouns (*their*) which are non-gender specific.

### Sexist:

**Everybody should take his book home.**
**Every American should know his rights.**

### Nonsexist:

**Everybody should take his or her book home.**

Or

**All the students** should take **their** books home.

**Every American** should know **his or her** rights.

Or

**All Americans** should know **their** rights.

Another acceptable means of avoiding sexist language is to alternate using masculine and feminine pronouns throughout the entire paper.

In general, be sensitive in your writing—both in the overall content and in the choice of individual words—to all points of view and to all groups of people. In so doing, you will be acting in an ethical and moral fashion. You will also earn a reputation as a fair, considerate, and careful writer.

# Appendix A: Sample Outline

I. Introduction
   A. Emphasis in the poem on surface appearances
   B. Thesis Statement: Gawain, making judgments based solely on outer appearances, misperceives those around him, his situation, and himself.

II. The Court's Stress on Outer Appearances
   A. Green Knight's dramatic entrance and the Court's wonder at "His hue most strange to see"
   B. Detailed description of the Green Knight's appearance
   C. The Court's false conclusions
      1. Deem him "phantom and faerie"
      2. Arthur ready for a fight

III. Early Clues Things Are Not What They Seem
   A. Repetition of how things "seemed" in the Green Knight's appearance
      1. It "seemed" no one could withstand his blows
      2. His hue "seemed" greener than green
   B. Guenevere's false "flawless" exterior
   C. Other members of Camelot put on false faces
      1. Arthur let "no sign be seen" of his concern
      2. Other courtiers "covered their care"
      3. Gawain hides his concern beneath "countenance glad"

IV. Gawain's Errors Based on Surface Appearances
   A. Gawain's arrival at Bercilak's Castle
      1. Describes in detail the castle's outside
      2. Thinks it a "paper castle" and sees no threat
   B. Later arrival at the Green Chapel
   C. Host "seemed" well suited to Gawain

V. Gawain Taken by Beauty of the Host's Wife
   A. Comparison of Lady to the crone
   B. Gawain's appreciation of the Lady's physical beauty
   C. Parallel of the hunt and the bedroom

VI. The Lady Leads to Trouble for Gawain
   A. Lady compared to Guenevere
   B. Lady keeps Gawain from noticing dangers
      1. Gawain never questions what she tells him
      2. Gawain never realizes the old woman is Morgan
   C. Acceptance of the Girdle
      1. Gawain trusts what the Lady tells him
      2. Girdle not what it "seems"

VII. Gawain Not What He Seems
   A. Chivalric Code and the Pentangle Shield
      1. Shield represents the code Gawain lives by
      2. Derek Hughes notes that Gawain's virtues are described in "metaphors of ornament and clothing" (222)
   B. Gawain's failings made known in Green Chapel
   C. Shield masks hidden flaw
      1. Shield worn on outside, "in sight" and "in view"
      2. Girdle is concealed
   D. Gawain's failure to recognize his own human fallibility

VIII. Conclusion
   A. Gawain's inner flaws revealed
   B. Other revelations in the poem prove appearances deceptive

# Appendix B: Sample Paper

Things Are Not What They Seem:
Deceptive Appearances in *Sir Gawain and the Green Knight*

By Random Student
Medieval Literature I
April 25, 1993

A great deal of the critical material concerning Sir Gawain and the Green Knight has addressed the nature of the test devised by the Green Knight and Morgan le Fay and the reasons why Gawain fails it.[1] One of the main reasons Gawain fails the test, however, is that he does not recognize he is being tested. Only when the Green Knight reveals his true identity does Gawain discover that the people and events in Bercilak's castle were not who and what they seemed. Throughout the poem, the poet stresses in his narration how things appear, particularly to the

---

[1] For different discussions of Gawain's testing, see Spearing (191–219); Markman (170–75); Morgan (58–59); Hunt (12–15); Henry (192–94); and Green (184).

*Introduction*

*General Statement (Notes a critical trend.)*

↓

*Narrows Down*

*Thesis Statement* — members of Camelot and to Gawain, their representative in the outer world, while hinting that appearances can be deceiving.[2] In so doing, the poet demonstrates that the courtiers and Gawain place great emphasis on superficial details, without ever considering or appreciating what may lie beneath the surface. This tendency ultimately contributes to Gawain's failure of the test, as he, making judgments based solely on outer appearances, misperceives those around him, his situation, and most important, himself.

*The Body*

*Topic Sentence*

*Body begins with broad principles, lays firm foundation.*

*Extensive quoting from primary source.*

*Summary Statement*

In his portrayal of Camelot, the poet demonstrates how the court gives great weight to outer appearances. The opening portrait is of a younger, more innocent Camelot (Spearing 181; Hunt 3), when "life was sweet" (line 49), "all this fair folk in their first age were still" (54–55), and Arthur was "a little boyish" (86).[3] Part of this innocence is a childlike wonder and delight in spectacular sights that becomes evident when the Green Knight makes his dramatic entrance. As the narrator describes, "Great wonder grew in hall/At his hue most strange to see" (148–49), and "Such a mount in his might, nor man on him riding,/None had seen, I dare swear, with sight in that hall so grand" (196–97). The narrator thereby describes how the Green Knight appears in the eyes of the court, stressing that it is the sight of him, more than anything else, that makes an impression on them.

*Links Paragraphs*

*Demonstrates Knowledge of the field.*

Significantly, the poet inserts a lengthy description of the Green Knight and his horse between these two references to how the Green Knight's appearance affects the court. By placing this description here, the poet indicates that the passage specifies aspects of the Green Knight that attract the court's notice. The Gawain poet often includes these lengthy descriptive passages, and while this stylistic trait could be discounted as merely fulfilling medieval convention, the poet also employs it for the-

*Bibliographic and Content Notes (To clarify and evaluate sources.)*

[2] Hughes does discuss the emphasis on surface appearances in the poem, particularly how the poet opposes artifice and ornament to true values and virtues (219), and notes how Gawain is "at the mercy of appearances" throughout the poem (232). While Hughes does mention that the poet's use of phrases such as "wyth syght" probably has some "relevance to the poem's design" (234), he does not analyze the places in which these phrases appear and thereby ignores many of the examples that I discuss, such as the poet's repeated description of how things "seem" to appear.

[3] For the purpose of clarity, I have chosen to use Marie Borroff's verse translation in quoting from the poem, indicating the line numbers in parentheses. I have checked the citations with the orginal Middle English text in order to ensure that the overall meaning remains consistent, particularly with respect to individual words such as "syght" and "semed."

104   A+ Term Papers

matic purposes (Spearing 177; Hughes 234). The extreme attention to detail here, as the narrator delights in describing the Knight's rich clothing, his "furs cut and fitted," "trim hose," "silk bands," "footgear well-fashioned," and "bright gems... richly ranged" (151–202), demonstrates how the court is attracted to only the most decorous and superficial features (Hughes 216–19). Moreover, several times throughout the description, the poet stresses the green coloring of the knight and his attire. Color, an especially shallow descriptive trait, so dominates the court's eyes it seems to blind them to more substantial characteristics. Although the poet initially indicates that the Green Knight is "formed with every feature in fair accord" (145), the court does not appreciate his fairness; it is "his hue most strange to see" that causes "wonder" in the hall, "For man and gear and all/Were green as green could be" (147–50).

After the Green Knight demands to see the captain of the court, receiving "stares on all sides... For much did they marvel what it might mean" (232–33), the narrator again stresses how the sight of the Knight affects the court:

> All the onlookers eyed him, and edged nearer,
> And awaited in wonder what he would do,
> For many sights had they seen, but such a one never,
> So that phantom and faerie the folk there deemed it.
> (231–40)

This passage also demonstrates how the court's emphasis on outer appearance leads them to draw faulty conclusions. As they had never seen a sight such as this one before, they quickly label it "phantom and faerie." In the end, however, we learn that, while some magic contributed to shaping the Green Knight's outer form, he is at heart a mortal. Yet the court's initial labeling of the Green Knight as "phantom and faerie" colors Gawain's conception of him and determines his future actions. Had Gawain considered that the Green Knight was mortal, he probably would not have resorted to a magic charm to protect himself. Similarly, despite the Green Knight's insistence that he means no harm, claiming that he "pass[es] here in peace and would part friends" (266), Arthur, perhaps taken in by his mighty stature, assumes the Green Knight is looking for a fight, telling him, "If contest here you crave,/You shall not fail to fight" (277–78).

*Analysis of a key passage.*

*Significant Passage Quoted and Set Apart...*

*...and Analyzed*

*Makes a supposition from another point of view*

*Topic Sentence (Links Paragraphs)*

↑

*Brings in examples to support assertion.*

↓

*Conclusion Drawn From Examples*

*Topic Sentence*

*Brings in critics, research for support.*

*Topic Sentence (Links Paragraphs)*

As these examples indicate, the poet, in these early parts of the poem, includes subtle warnings to his audience that things are not what they appear, foreshadowing the revelations in the Green Chapel. For example, when the narrator says of the Green Knight, "As lightning quick and light/He looked to all at hand;/It seemed that no man might/His deadly dints withstand" (199–202), he does not conclusively state that the Knight is all-powerful, only that it "seemed" so. This assessment, again based on the Green Knight's appearance, proves faulty, as Gawain does in the end withstand a blow from him. Similarly, the narrator says that the Knight's hue was "greener, it seemed,/Than green fused on gold more glorious by far" (234–35). By repeatedly describing how the Green Knight "seemed" to appear, the narrator indicates that we are viewing the Knight not from an objective, omniscient perspective but from the point of view of human onlookers, presumably the courtiers, whose observations must remain confined to surface details. Moreover, the word "seemed" implies a degree of uncertainty in the description, indicating that things may not, in fact, be what they seem.

The narrator includes other sly indications that outer appearances may be deceiving. As he does with the Green Knight, the narrator's first description of Guinevere emphasizes how she appears to onlookers: "Fair queen, without a flaw,/She glanced with eyes of grey./A seemlier that once he saw,/In truth, no man can say" (80–83). While Guinevere may appear flawless to those observing her within the poem, she would not seem so spotless to the poem's contemporary audience. As Albert Friedman points out, the Gawain Poet was certainly acquainted with the great French romances (144), and his audience probably knew of Guinevere's besmirched reputation. To them, her seemly appearance merely disguises deceit and cunning brewing within. In a similar manner, as Tony Hunt describes, the poet refers in the poem's opening to Aeneas, who, like Guinevere, was a trusted member of court, but eventually revealed as a traitor.[4]

In addition to Guinevere, other members of Camelot display false faces that mask their inner selves. For example, the narrator says that Arthur "at heart had wonder" about the Green Knight, but "he let no sign be seen" (467–68) and proceeds to

---

[4]While Hunt discusses the treachery of Aeneas, Borroff, in a footnote to her translation, describes Antenor as the deceitful knight (1). In either case, the treachery remained unknown, supporting my argument that the opening of the poem establishes how appearances are deceiving.

offer words of comfort to the queen. Similarly, the beginning of Gawain's journey in the second part carries a reminder of this kind of hypocrisy; although the court felt "sorrow" for Gawain and were "sore at heart," they "covered their care with countenance glad:/Many a mournful man made mirth for his sake" (541–42). Gawain himself puts on an outer display contrary to his inner emotions, making light of the Green Knight's visit despite its ominous implications that the narrator stresses are understood by everyone: "The king and Gawain gay/Make game of the Green Knight there,/Yet all who saw it say/'Twas a wonder past compare" (465–66). Similarly, when Gawain departs, he makes a great display of courage, saying that, "The terms of this task too well you know—To count the cost over concerns me nothing" (546–47) and asking with a smile and tranquil eye, "Why should I tarry?.... In destinies sad or merry,/True men can but try" (561–64). By describing this departure within the same stanza in which he mentions the court covering its concern behind "countenance glad," the poet links the two scenes together, hinting that Gawain's seeming bravery may also mask "secret sorrow" and fear. As the Green Knight eventually reveals, Gawain does indeed have great concern for his life.

When Gawain sets out on his journey, he does so as a true representative of Camelot, rating his circumstances based solely upon outer appearances and thereby making critical errors in judgment that determine his fate. For example, when Gawain first arrives at Bercilak's castle, the narrator includes an intricate descriptive passage, as Gawain "stared at that stronghold great/As it shimmered and shone amid shining leaves" (771–72). Again, as with the Green Knight, the passage particularly emphasizes the most external details, describing the moat, the bridge, the gate, and the outer wall. As the courtiers at Camelot did, Gawain makes a judgment based upon his observations of these superficial attributes. Describing the pinnacles that "vied there for [Gawain's] view," the narrator notes, "verily it seemed/A castle cut of paper for a king's feast" (801–2), indicating how in Gawain's eyes, the castle attains a fairy tale-like perfection that poses no substantial threat. Based on what he sees, Gawain deems the castle "fair and bright" and a safe place for him to reside. However, the narrator, as before, uses the word "seemed," warning that the "paper castle" may in fact hold more dangers than at first appears. Gawain's arrival here parallels his arrival at the Green Chapel in the final section.

*Examples, quotations brought in.*

*Summary Statement (Draws a conclusion)*

*After laying the foundation, the argument moves on to more specific and complex points.*

*However, it still ties new points to earlier ones.*

*Makes a comparison.*

Again, the narrator describes Gawain's perception of the location, relating how Gawain, looking "for a sight of the Chapel," finds that "no such place appeared which puzzled him sore,/Yet he saw some way off what seemed like a mound" (2169–71). Based on the bleak scene, Gawain labels the Green Chapel "hideous" and "accursed," a place where "might/the devil himself be seen" and comes to believe that it is actually the "Fiend" who has tempted him (2185–195). Ironically, he does not realize that this hellish scene actually holds no danger for him; his fate has already been determined in the seemingly innocent "castle cut of paper."

*Topic Sentence (Links Paragraphs)*

Gawain makes a similar mistake in perception when he first meets his host. As with the castle itself, the host is subjected to an examination by Gawain but, again, one that never penetrates beneath the surface: "Gawain gazed on the host that greeted him there,/And a lusty fellow he looked, the lord of that place" (843–44). Gawain quickly makes judgments based on what he sees, as the narrator notes, "well suited [the host] seemed in Sir Gawain's sight/To be a master of men in a mighty keep" (848–49). Stressing that this is a subjective description of the host confined to "Gawain's sight," the poet again interjects the word "seemed," slyly hinting that he may not, in reality, be the hearty host that he seems in Gawain's eyes. Not subjecting his host to more careful scrutiny, Gawain never suspects Bercilak's secret, more threatening, identity.

*Topic Sentence Argument moves on to make a key point related to the thesis.*

Gawain's regard for outer appearance plays an especially critical role in his relationship with the host's wife. From the moment that Gawain first meets the lady, the narrator emphasizes how conscious Gawain is of her beauty: "The fair hues of her flesh, her face and her hair/And her body and her bearing were beyond praise . . . as Sir Gawain thought" (943–45). Gawain's appreciation of physical beauty is further emphasized by the elaborate 19-line comparison between the lady and the "crone" who accompanies her. The passage emphasizes the women's physical appearances, noting that they are "unlike to look upon" (950), and detailing the differences in their attire, skin tone, muscle build, and facial features. While Gawain finds the old woman "unsightly to see," he becomes more attracted to "the beauty by her side" (963–69) and ultimately "gaze[s]" solely upon "that gay lady" (970).

*Transitional sentence to bridge ideas*

The lady's attempted seduction of Gawain, from her first entrance into his bedroom in which she is described as "loveliest to behold" (1187) to her "sweet stolen glances, that stirred his stout heart" (1659), is grounded in his continual awareness and appreciation of her physical appearance. The alternation between the bedroom and the hunt particularly demonstrates the important role that appearance and sight plays in Gawain's temptation. As many critics have noted, the poet, in paralleling the bedroom and hunting scenes, establishes a variety of contrasts, between the masculine, violent outer world of the hunt and the softer, feminine inside world of the bedroom.[5] The scenes also evidence a contrast between the senses of sight and sound. Although the hunt does feature some references to how things appear, the descriptions are overwhelmingly dominated by sound, as in the following passage:

> When the hounds opened cry, the head of the hunt
> Rallied them with rough words, raised a great noise.
> The hounds that had heard it came hurrying straight
> And following along with their fellows, forty together.
> Then such a clamor and cry of coursing hounds
> Arose, that the rocks resounded again.
> Hunters exhorted them with horn and with voice....
> (1422–28)

In contrast, Gawain's bedroom meetings with the lady increasingly stress the sense of sight, particularly how she appears in his eyes:

> But when he sees her at his side he summons his wits,
> Breaks from the black dreams and blithely answers.
>
> ...........................................
>
> He sees her so glorious, so gaily attired,
> So faultless her features, so fair and so bright,
>
> His heart swelled swiftly with surging joys.
> They melt into mirth with many a fond smile,
> And there was bliss beyond telling between those two,
>     at height.
>         Good were their words of greeting;
>         Each joyed in other's sight;
>         Great peril attends that meeting
>         Should Mary forget her knight. (1755–69)

*Topic Sentence*

*Notes a critical trend.*

*Gives new perspective of a standard interpretation.*

*Passages Quoted, Set Apart, Compared, and Analyzed*

---

[5] For discussions of the hunting and temptation scenes, see Spearing (212–19); Hunt (12–13); and Henry (188–89). Spearing (213) and Henry (189) also both note that sound is a prominent sense in the hunting scenes, but oppose it to the silence of the bedroom, rather than to the sense of sight, as I do.

*Topic Sentence (Links to previous paragraph)*

↑

*Analysis of the primary source*

↓

*Summary Statement*

*Writer lays out the significance of this point for the reader...*

*...and then develops it further*

*Establishes a pattern*

*Bridge to other significant points to be made*

Gawain, entranced by the lady's exterior beauty, unwittingly places himself in "great peril" in several crucial areas. In the passage quoted above, the lady is described as "faultless," mirroring the earlier description of Guinevere, "queen, without a flaw" (81), and Gawain himself directly compares the two women, thinking the lady's attributes "excelled the queen herself" (945). Like Guinevere, the lady's "faultless" exterior disguises a treacherous interior. While the reader senses that Gawain is in some greater danger, Gawain, although he recognizes that the lady hopes to seduce him, fails to question her motives more carefully and therefore never considers her part in a greater plot being acted against him. He fully accepts her claim that no one knows of her visits to his chamber, not suspecting that she is reporting the events back to her husband. More seriously, Gawain's attraction to the lady distracts him from noticing a greater peril. In the first passage in which the lady is compared to her "ancient" companion, Gawain appears so taken by the beauty of the lady that he tends to discount the older woman. Declaring the old woman's features "unsightly to see" (963), Gawain finds "More toothsome, to his taste,/Was the beauty by her side," whom he proceeds to "gaze" upon (968–70). Gawain thereby concentrates his attention on the beautiful lady while relegating the crone to the sidelines, rendering her almost invisible. This proves a critical mistake, however, as the old woman is really Morgan le Fay, the mastermind behind the plot to test him and the court. Gawain never suspects that this "unsightly" person is not only his own aunt, but in control of his destiny.

Gawain's failure to consider his situation more carefully leads to his acceptance of the lady's girdle, an action that plays an important part in determining his fate.... When Gawain initially refuses to accept the girdle, the lady questions if he does so "Because it seems in your sight so simple a thing?" (1847). The lady thereby specifically warns Gawain that outer appearances can be deceiving, the word "seems," as it does throughout the poem, implying a hidden meaning beneath the surface. The girdle is indeed not as "simple" as it "seems," and the lady proceeds to make "known" the hidden "virtue that invests it," the girdle's magical ability to protect the wearer from all peril (1849–50). But the girdle is more than it seems in other ways; not only a magic charm but also the centerpiece in Gawain's testing that, unbeknownst to him, will become the mark of his "failings" in the Green Chapel.

The events in the Green Chapel reveal that Gawain, like the people and situations he encounters, bears a somewhat deceptive outer appearance. When Gawain initially sets out on his quest, the narrator establishes him as the epitome of the chivalric knight,[6] committed to the values and virtues as they are represented by the Pentangle on his shield (Spearing 175, 179). As several critics have discussed, the Pentangle becomes a sign of the standard of perfection and knightly virtue with which Gawain aligns himself.[7] Yet as the Pentangle is imprinted on Gawain's shield, it serves as a part of his armor and is therefore confined to his outer person. As Derek Hughes argues, by describing Gawain's virtues not as internal qualities but "in metaphors of ornament and clothing," the narrator "hints that Gawain's hold on his ideals is not as firm as it might be" (222). Significantly, the narrator discusses the Pentangle within a lengthy descriptive passage about Gawain's armor and attire. As he did with the Green Knight in the first section of the poem, the poet describes Gawain's "goodly gear" with careful attention to the fine and intricate details, such as the "Turkestan silk," "lustrous fur," "finest gold," and "best cloth" (566–618). Thus the Pentangle, as well as the code it signifies, becomes merely another superficial ornament that, as with the Green Knight's deceptive outer shape, does not necessarily reflect the inner person.

In the Green Chapel, Gawain's seeming perfection and virtue are indeed revealed to belie a "faulty and false" interior, as his hidden "failings" are "made known" to him (2391). The exact nature of these "failings" remains somewhat ambiguous in the poem, as the poet offers several possible faults (Spearing 208–9, 220–22). While the Green Knight says that Gawain has acted because he understandably "loved [his] own life" (2368), Gawain criticizes himself not only for his "care for [his] life," but also for cowardice, frailty of the flesh, covetousness, and falsehood (2378–83; 2435). No matter the exact nature of his fault, however, Gawain's acceptance of the girdle betrays a weakness that, although understandably human, is a breach of the chivalric code, creating a dent in his shield.[8] In contrast to

---

[6]Spearing (175), Markman (162), and Green (177) all describe Gawain as representing some form of the ideal chivalric or Christian Knight.
[7]Several critics address the symbolism of the shield and Pentangle. See Spearing (197–98); Howard (196–201); Henry (194); Green (176–94); and Hughes (222). Green and Hughes also note how the narrator's description of the Pentangle includes subtle hints that Gawain's devotion to these virtues is not as firm as it might appear.
[8]Spearing is particularly good on this, noting that the "endless knot" of the Pentangle's virtues does not allow any point to have a failing without destroying the whole (198, 228),

*Topic Sentence (sums up a key point) critic brought in for support*

*Summary Statement (Draws a conclusion that is a key point in the argument)*

the shield, the emblem of knightly virtue, the girdle thereby becomes an emblem of Gawain's fault (Howard 199).[9]

The shield thereby serves to mask in Gawain the fallibility and imperfection that exists in all of us. As A. C. Spearing points out, in aligning himself with the Pentangle, Gawain sets his sights on a perfection that is humanly unattainable (228). Until the events in the Green Chapel make his failings known to him, however, Gawain refuses to acknowledge this human fallibility within himself.[10] In contrast to the shield, which Gawain wears "in sight" and "in view" (635–36), the narrator stresses that the girdle is initially concealed from view, as the lady insists that Gawain "conceal it well,/Lest the noble lord should know" and Gawain agrees, "That not a soul save themselves shall see it thenceforth with sight" (1862–65). Significantly, Gawain is punished not so much for accepting the girdle as for concealing it; while he receives only feigned blows for the two kisses he "restored," he is nicked for the "third throw" when he "lacked . . . a little in loyalty" (2366) and did not turn over the girdle to his host.[11] In being punished for not revealing the girdle, Gawain, in a sense, is also punished for not admitting to his own humanity, which has remained hidden beneath a glittering, yet superficial, standard of perfection. His failure of the test thereby results from his inability to peer beneath the surface not only of his situation and companions, but also himself.

and that Gawain's experiences bring out the "instability" of this balance of virtues and values (201).

[9]Howard's essay thoroughly compares and contrasts the girdle and the shield. Also see Henry (194). Morgan also discusses them, but does not contrast them, instead saying that the girdle "renders explicit the sinfulness implicit in the definition of human perfection" represented by the shield (146). While I agree that the girdle is a sign of imperfection, I do not see the Pentangle as a symbol of "human" perfection, but as a symbol of perfection that is humanly unattainable.

[10]Green (184–85), Markman (170, 175), Morgan (59), and Henry (194) all describe how Gawain's testing reveals his human imperfection and fallibility. Markman, however, goes too far in excusing Gawain, claiming that Gawain is seen as a "splendid man" who "passes his tests" and "shows us our capabilities for human conduct, because, in the best sense of it, he shows us what honest moral conduct is" (175). Gawain's unwillingness to admit to his fallibility indicates an unattractive lack of humility for which he seems to be punished in the Green Chapel, and for which he condemns himself, keeping the girdle, he says, to "lower my pride" (2438).

[11]Markman claims Gawain's loyalty is a major aspect of the poem (164–65; 172, 173). However, I have to disagree when Markman says that Gawain remains loyal to Bercilak (164) and that he receives the nick because he made the "slightest compromise" (173). While it is true that he is "loyal" in not having sexual relations with Bercilak's wife, Gawain's acceptance of the girdle is presented by the Green Knight as a breach in loyalty. I also realize that one could then argue that Gawain receives the blow primarily for this disloyalty to his host. However, the nature of his disloyalty is not his having had sexual relations with the lady, nor his acceptance of her girdle, but that he has concealed the girdle, thereby placing it in the context of deceptive appearances that run throughout the poem.

## Conclusion

*Affirms Thesis*

The Green Chapel is a place of manifold revelations, in which the earlier foreshadowings that things are not what they seem are proven accurate. Not only are the true identities of the Green Knight, the alluring temptress, and her ancient companion revealed, but a part of Gawain is uncovered as well. His "failings made known" (2391), Gawain finds his protective armor stripped away, revealing the humanity that has existed beneath the surface all along. It is appropriate that in this poem of exchanges, the girdle, the symbol of Gawain's fault and imperfection that had previously been hidden, ultimately becomes fixed to his outer person. In addition to his actual battle scar, Gawain returns to Camelot displaying the girdle, as he says to the court, "Behold. . . . the blazon of the blemish that I bear on my neck . . . I must bear it on my body until I breathe my last" (2505–10). He also seems to return with an understanding of both the deceptive nature of appearances and the futility of living by a code of unattainable perfection that masks one's humanity. As he says in his final words, "For one may keep a deed dark, but undo it no whit,/For where a fault is made fast, it is fixed evermore" (2511–12).

*Nonstandard Conclusion: Introduces a new point that relates to and emerges from the proven thesis.*

# Appendix C: Sample Bibliography

## Works Cited

**PRIMARY SOURCE**

*Sir Gawain and the Green Knight*. Trans. Marie Borroff. New York: Norton, 1967.

**SECONDARY SOURCES**

Blanch, Robert J., ed. *Sir Gawain and Pearl: Critical Essays*. Bloomington: Indiana University Press, 1966.

Friedman, Albert B. "Morgan le Fay in *Sir Gawain and the Green Knight*." Blanch 135–58.

Green, Richard Hamilton. "Gawain's Shield and the Quest for Perfection." Blanch 176–94.

Henry, Avril. "Temptation and Hunt in *Sir Gawain and the Green Knight*." *Medium Aevum* 45.2 (1976):187–99.

Howard, Donald R. "Structure and Symmetry in Sir Gawain." Blanch 195–208.

Hughes, Derek W. "The Problem of Reality in *Sir Gawain and the Green Knight*." *University of Toronto Quarterly* 40 (1971):217–235.

Hunt, Tony. "Irony and Ambiguity in *Sir Gawain and the Green Knight*." *Forum for Modern Language Studies* 12.1 (1976):1–16.

Markman, Alan M. "The Meaning of *Sir Gawain and the Green Knight*." Blanch 159–75.

Morgan, Gerald. Sir Gawain and the Green Knight *and the Idea of Righteousness*. Dublin: Irish Academic Press, 1991.

Spearing, A. C. *The Gawain-Poet: A Critical Study*. Cambridge: The Cambridge University Press, 1970.

# Glossary

**abstract:** a type of index that includes brief descriptions or excerpts from each article listed.

**annotated bibliography:** a listing of various sources that includes a brief summary of each one.

**anthology:** a collection of articles, essays, or other literary works, usually bound together within a single volume.

**antecedent:** a word or phrase to which a pronoun refers.

**bibliographic note:** a supplementary note that appears either as a footnote at the bottom of the page or at the end of the research paper listing several sources that refer to or support a statement made in the text; provides additional bibliographic information about sources that may be too extensive to fit in a parenthetical reference.

**bibliography:** a listing of all sources referred to in the paper, detailing complete publication information for each; also, a listing of sources relating to a particular subject (similar to the Works Cited, but lists only print sources).

**bibliography card:** an index card filled out for the writer's own benefit during the research process that details publication information about a single source; used to help in the organization of the paper's bibliography.

**body:** the bulk of a research paper, consisting of all the text between the introduction and the conclusion.

**call number:** a combination of letters and numbers assigned to each book in the library that is used to help locate the book within the library. It will appear both in the catalog entry and on the book itself.

**card catalog:** the library's index of all its books, kept on cards that are usually alphabetized and separated according to author, title, and subject. Each card will display the call number and information about the book.

**citation:** an entry in a bibliography or a documentation of a source in a research paper that shows key information about the source.

**cliché:** a trite word or expression that has been used so frequently it is now commonplace; should be avoided in writing research papers.

**colloquialism:** a word or expression used in casual and informal conversation.

**conclusion:** the final paragraph or paragraphs of a research paper that often restates and reaffirms the paper's main points.

**content note:** a supplementary note that appears either as a footnote at the bottom of the page or at the end of the research paper and provides additional information to or explanations of what has been discussed in the text of the paper; used to clarify a point of view, to provide additional background information, to evaluate various sources in more detail, or to take issue with a particular source or point of view.

**Dewey decimal system:** a system of classification commonly used in libraries by which each title in the library is given a number indicating its general subject and location in the library.

**ellipsis:** three spaced dots used to indicate the omission of a word or words from a quoted passage of text (when the omission comes at the end of the sentence, four spaced periods are used).

**homophone:** a word that sounds like another but is spelled differently and carries a different definition.

**independent clause:** a group of words that includes a subject and verb and is able to stand on its own as a complete sentence.

**index:** a listing of various sources on a single topic, primarily for journal and magazine articles and essays within larger works.

**infinitive:** a form of a verb that is preceded by the word *to;* it is usually considered poor grammar to split an infinitive by placing another word between *to* and the second part of the verb.

**introduction:** the opening paragraph(s) of a research paper in which the main idea is set up and introduced.

**Library of Congress subject headings:** topics established by the Library of Congress that most libraries use to designate books in their subject catalogs.

**Library of Congress system:** a system of classification used in many libraries by which each title in the library is given a combination of letters and numbers to indicate its general subject and location in the library.

**microform:** a process by which a piece of printed material is reduced to a smaller size and saved on film, usually either microfilm (a long strip) or microfiche (a single sheet).

**modifier:** a word or phrase that describes or elaborates upon some other word.

**note card:** an index card that lists one specific piece of information derived from a source; used solely for the writer's own benefit to help in the preparation, organization, and writing of a research paper.

**on-line catalog:** the library's index of all its books kept on computer database, enabling users to search by author, title, and subject, and often indicating the book's status.

**outline:** a list of the main points in the paper, divided into categories and subcategories and put in approximate order, used to help organize the paper.

**paraphrase:** a restatement of the main ideas of a textual passage, rephrased in different terms.

**parenthetical reference:** an abbreviated documentation (usually the author's last name or the source's title) that appears in the text of the paper in parentheses and indicates which source the information came from and exactly where in the source it was found. It will correspond to a listing in the Works Cited that details the full publication information.

**passive construction:** a verbal phrase made up of any form of the verb *to be* and another verb.

**periodical:** a publication, such as a magazine or journal, that is published at fixed intervals of time.

**plagiarism:** the act of passing off someone else's ideas or writing as one's own without giving the original writer credit; considered a crime and a serious breach of ethics.

**preposition:** words in the English language that normally appear at the beginning of a phrase and are used to describe or to elaborate upon some other word in the sentence. It is generally considered poor grammar to end a sentence with a preposition.

**primary source:** original documents that are often the main focus of a paper, such as works of literature, historical documents, essays, and articles on certain theories and philosophies, or data obtained in a scientific study.

**pronoun:** a word that takes the place of a noun (such as *he, she, it,* etc.).

**quotation:** an exact restatement of a passage of text using the same words and punctuation as the original.

**reference books:** informational books that may not be checked out of the library and must be consulted within the library.

**run-on sentence:** a sentence that contains too many clauses or phrases, often serving to confuse the reader.

**secondary sources:** books or articles by critics, historians, scholars, or other writers that comment upon, address, and analyze primary sources.

**sentence fragment:** a group of words that does not function as a complete sentence, usually lacking a subject or verb and therefore unable to stand on its own.

**slang:** words or expressions that are not considered standard English but have fallen into popular usage; nonformal, nonstandard words and language, usually popular among a certain group or during a certain period of time.

**subordinate clause:** a full sentence pattern that functions within a sentence as an adjective, an adverb, or noun but cannot stand alone as a complete sentence.

**synonym:** a word or expression that has the same meaning as another word.

**thesaurus:** a type of dictionary that lists words and their synonyms.

**thesis statement:** the paper's main idea, usually some kind of theory, argument, or viewpoint relating to a particular topic that is proven in the body of the paper.

**topic sentence:** a sentence, usually the first in a paragraph, that summarizes or introduces the main idea of the paragraph.

**transition:** a word, phrase, or sentence used to link different ideas together, providing smoother flow in the text.

**working bibliography:** a list of sources to be examined for possible use in the paper that, upon being narrowed down during the researching and writing of the paper, will eventually become the final bibliography; used solely for the writer's own benefit to aid in the research process.

**Works Cited:** a listing of all the sources referred to in the paper, detailing complete publication information for each (similar to the bibliography, but lists both print and nonprint sources).